Emotional Intelligence in Conflicts

Emotional Intelligence in Conflicts

J.D. Román

Manuel Ferrández

www.librosenred.com

C.E.O.: Marcelo Perazolo
Cover Design: Daniela Ferrán
Interior Design: Julieta Mariatti

Copyright © 2012 LibrosEnRed

All rights reserved, including the right to reproduce this book or any part thereof in any form, except for inclusion of brief quotations in a review, without the written permission of the publisher.

Design, typesetting, and other prepress work by LibrosEnRed
www.librosenred.com

ISBN: 978-1-59754-851-9
First English Edition - Print on Demand

LibrosEnRed©
A trade mark of Amertown International S.A.
editorial@librosenred.com

"The man who wants to do something always finds a way; the man who doesn't want to do anything always finds an excuse".

Chinese proverb

"Pick battles big enough to matter, but small enough to win".

Jonathan Kozol

Table of contents

Introduction — 9

Part 1
The conflict and its peculiarities — 17

What is conflict? — 19

Diagnose the disagreements — 25
   A – Nature of the disagreement — 25
   B – Underlying factors — 27
      Tale of the six wise blind men and the elephant — 28

The four stages of the conflict — 32
   Stage 1: The latent conflict — 32
   Stage 2: The perceived conflict — 33
   Stage 3: The conflict "felt" — 34
   Stage 4: The expressed conflict — 34

Sources of conflict (detail) — 37
   The inference ladder — 38

Levels of conflict — 43
   A – Intrapersonal conflict — 43
   B – Interpersonal conflict — 44

Stages of the process	44
C – Intragroup conflict	45
D – Intergroup conflict	45
Is conflict bad?	**47**
Negative aspects of the conflict	48
Costs of the conflict	49
The conflict can be constructive when …	49
Conflict and performance	**53**
Conflict and performance organizational	54
The dramatic triangle	**55**
The persecutor (attacking)	58
The savior	58
The victim	60
Who's the culprit?	63
Personal styles to confront the conflict	**67**
1 – Imposition	68
2 – To elude	70
3 – To accommodate (submission)	72
4 – To collaborate	73
5 – To yield (or better put "to bargain" or "compromise")	75
Understanding the conflict	**79**
Power and self-esteem	80
Power	81
Self esteem	81
Structure and dynamics of the conflict	82
People	83

The process	84
The problem	85
Characteristics of the conflicts	87
Modality	90

Part 2
The positive management of conflicts — 93

Why are conflicts unwished?	95
Actions not to be taken	100
"Old" brain vs "new" brain	105
Simplified Transactional analysis	109
Assertiveness: a key skill	111
How to transmit that we are living a conflict?	117
Give information	117
To give our opinion or our point of view	118
To expose our needs and our desires	119
To expose our feelings	121
To explain our feelings	121
How to find out about the vision of "the Other" about the undergoing conflict?	123
Looking for information	123
To listen	124
Show empathy	126
Accept the critiques	127
The non-verbal communication in the conflicts	129

Elements of a cooperative process in conflicts solving	135
Communication in conflicts	139
Factors that favor communication:	139
Messages that hamper communication:	140
Request changes of behavior	141
Stage 1: Detect the problem	142
Stage 2: Expose that we have a problem	143
Stage 3: Make him see the impact of its behavior	144
Stage 4: Describe how we feel	144
Stage 5: Listen to the point of view of the interlocutor	145
Stage 6: Ask for the wished behavior	146
Stage 7: Resolution	147
LibrosEnRed Publishing House	**151**

Introduction

Conflict is one of the most powerful human interactions. It can propitiate personal growth as well as damage the involved actors. Probably due to its biased utilization, the word "conflict" has become a cursed word, with numerous negative connotations. Popularly, there is many a confusion over the meaning and the purpose of the conflict.

Many persons think, not lacking reason, that conflict is negative and even highly destructive. For example, at our workplace, troubled relations along with their ineffective management constitute one of the most important stress generators. The conflict affects not only the quality of work life, but also the productivity of the whole organization.

In fact, some surveys tell us that managers dedicate roughly more than 20 % of their time to managing conflicts and to looking for solutions to anticipate them or to minimize their negative effects.

All in all, this negative vision of the conflict is only one of the possible perspectives. Actually conflict can be a positive drive for the development of our inner strengths and sense of purpose, or for the triggering of personal development action plans.

The presence of conflicts is an inevitable, and actually a necessary element to foment creativity, innovation and even team bonding, strange as it may seem. From this point of view, discrepancies constitute a magnificent opportunity to generate knowledge and to flee from the so-called "group-thinking" (where any individual thought is diluted within the crowd).

Precisely one of the intentions of this book is to analyze the consequences of the conflict and what are the factors and strategies that can minimize its negative consequences and what lines of action it is necessary to adopt to enjoy its benefits, which actually exist.

The best example is given by a standard team-building process, where in order to actually build a team, we have to go through a "conflict" stage, where all "pieces" may start fitting together. Even more, even shockingly so, whether that conflict would not appear, it is the duty of the team leader to sting the members so some latent frictions may evolve into an actual conflict situation.

We will not dwell on that specific use of provoked conflicts in team-building processes. We have already covered in depth such a complex and sensitive strategy in one of our books (The Paper Bridge).

Conflict, in any case, constitutes a daily reality. Be it at home or at work, our needs and values will invariably enter in opposition with those of other people, although the appearance of the conflict can be cloaked in various forms.

Some conflicts are relatively not important, easy to manage or even forgettable. Others though require an effective strategy for a successful resolution and to avoid a lasting hostility.

In order to make a distinction between the different types of conflicts, understanding the dynamics of their effects will be of great help. As we will cover later, disagreements on the content of a task or on the way of performing it (also including the differences in points of view, in ideas and in opinions), define the so-called conflict "of task".

On the other hand, the so-called conflict "of relations" has more to deal with the discrepancies and the incompatibilities that arise between people due to personal problems (not so much related to work, but to tastes, ideas or values). Almost always, this type of conflicts generates tension between the involved people, as well as some hostility feelings.

When we face a relational conflict we see that between the parts a dynamical process initiates where the involved persons experience negative emotional reactions because of some perceived discrepancies and interferences in the achievement of their aims. The conflict gives way to emotional and affective processes that provoke emotional states of anger, aggressiveness, grief, reproaches and resentment.

Because of that, the conflict requires of, as it happens with any other stressor, the generation of resources that help us minimize or annul the situation of discrepancy that takes place. In other words, we need an adaptive response before a situation of conflict.

When there is differences between persons and the latter don't possess the required resources to deal with the pressure cast upon them by their opponent, conflict turns into an important source of stress.

In the present book, we will analyze some preventive factors against the harmful effects of this type of conflict (such as the styles of conflict management or the mediation from third parties).

In our opinion, the skill of successfully solving conflicts is probably one of the most important skills that any person may master, and, at the same time, one of the most difficult to command. In practice, in fact, we have few formal opportunities to learn the skills of conflicts solving.

Nevertheless, we are fully convinced that, as any other human skill, conflicts solving can be taught and learned. As any other skill, it consists of a number of subskills, each one of them separated and interdependent. However, all those skills have to be assimilated first at the cognitive level, hence this book.

Starting with this premise, the intention of the present book is to put forward some tools that may help the reader command what we call "basic reflexes" when facing troubled situations. Especially, when we are exposed to unexpected troubled situations.

We are convinced that internalizing those basic reflexes will help the reader successfully face the above-mentioned situations.

The approach that we propose here is close to that used in some schools of martial arts where, instead of learning complex and somewhat unnatural moves, we take advantage of the natural reflexes of the human being in front of an aggression, through acquiring a series of simple although tremendously effective habits.

A very –albeit non-trivial– basic example: before any verbal aggression it is extremely effective to acquire the reflex of not answering reactively, i.e. of not speaking immediately.

At the root of this behaviour we find a vital premise that we need to have deeply ingrained when facing a conflict, any conflict: it is not possible to solve a conflict that resides in the emotional part of the brain. Therefore, the only possibility of being eventually successful when dealing with a conflict is splitting it into different parts and addressing those that dwell in the rational level of the mind.

Key sentence

Beliefs and values are located in the emotional part of the brain.

Any argument spinning solely around beliefs is doomed since its inception, and the conflict cannot meet a fruitful outcome, whatever the techniques we put into play.

As a collateral aspect, let's always bear in mind that conflict solving is not a "pissing contest" where only the strongest may win. The most transcendent thing in any conflict is the wished fair and satisfactory final outcome, and this aspect should be always born in mind.

This is especially true if we are drawn into a conflict on values and beliefs. We may feel relieved and satisfied after having exposed the said beliefs and fiercely standing for them with all our strength before our opponent, but we haven't moved a single step towards any hint of resolution.

At your local pub, a common and frivolous —or not that frivolous— example:

John: *"I believe ManU is the best team in the world"*

Mark: *" I strongly disagree, Arsenal are the best side in the world"*

Now we have a conflict of beliefs that may end up in a nice pub brawl. Both contenders will hold their grounds and no positive outcome whatsoever may be expected from that interaction. Here we are in the typical above-mentioned "pissing contest". Nothing to do with conflicts solving.

So a good initial question would be:" What's my objective: do I want to show off, do I want to vent out some frustration, do I want to influence my opponent, do I want to bring closure to a conflictive situation, etc …?"

The next question could then be: "Do I have the skills and tools to bring that conflict to a satisfactory end?"

If so, our fervent desire is that the reading of this book provides you with some useful models and skills for conflicts solving. Bear in mind that in the end:

- The conflicts appear when dealing with persons, with tasks and with ourselves.
- The indicators of conflict can be identified so soon as they appear.
- Some strategies may help us solve conflicts.

- Most conflicts can be minimized and, in many cases, solved.

Finally, remember that as in a tennis match for instance, in conflicts, coolness and mental strength constitute two crucial qualities if we want to prevail in the end.

Part 1
The conflict and its peculiarities

WHAT IS CONFLICT?

After having pored over the abundant existing bibliography on the topic, we have found numerous conceptualizations of the conflict. We might conclude that the term "conflict" turns out to be extremely blurred.

Some authors contemplate the existence of different types of conflict depending on the level of analysis used (later we will mention them: intrapersonal, interpersonal, intergroup, international, etc.) whereas, on the contrary, other authors support that independently of the level of analysis and the particular area where the conflict takes place (for example, with relatives, in an organization, etc.) the same conceptualization basically applies to all of them.

This way, for example, the "Journal of Conflict Resolution" pleads for the development of a general theory of the conflict, stating that:

"*Very expensive wars and domestic fights, to a great extent match the pattern of a regular armament race. Frustration generates aggression both at individual and country level. Jurisdictional problems of unions and territorial disputes between countries are not dissimilar*".

At the workplace, some authors mention the following basic elements to bear in mind when having to decide whether a situation might qualify or not as of conflict:

- 1.Interaction between two or more persons.
- 2.Existence of subjectively incompatible internal or external behaviors.
- 3.Premeditation in harming "the Other" (the opposite party), or, at least, attribution of such premeditation.
- 4.Direct or indirect utilization of power.
- 5.Normative inefficiency.

Of those five elements, in our opinion, the existence of a normative inefficiency acquires special relevancy, as it distinguishes the conflict from what might be a mere situation of competition.

In fact, many of the situations where a struggle for the reaching of an aim takes place between two people cannot be qualified as of conflict. As they take place within a given and concrete normative frame, where, in spite of the fact that obviously there is a dispute that will be solved in terms of a victor and of a loser, a previous agreement exists on the procedure that will rule the game. This peculiarity eliminates the potential sources of conflict.

In this type of situations, the conflict, would it exist, remains at an intrapersonal level consisting in agreeing with and justifying the reasons for the defeat (we will later detail that this level is precisely one of the levels where the conflict starts warming up).

On the other hand, it is very important to emphasize that we only need that one of the parts perceives the existence of subjectively incompatible behaviors and the attribution of premeditation for harming in order to place ourselves before a potential situation of conflict. As we will see, the conflict doesn't need of the presence of some objectively opposite interests.

Key sentence
Basically, the mere subjective perception of this incompatibility can lead to the triggering of a conflict.

Among the mentioned elements, to many authors the utilization of power seems to be intimately related to the definition of the conflict. For the Canadian Mintzberg, for example, power is having the aptitude of achieving some things to be done, of having some effect the on actions and decisions of the opposite parties.

This affirmation leads us again to the premises put forward at the beginning of this section: every agent (internal or external) has some power and a set of influences that he may deploy in order that his interests are attended and the corresponding resources are assigned to him.

Let's use an example in a managerial environment. The company is shaped by a system of authority (the flowchart) and the different groups (departments, teams, etc.) need a global coordination as they each struggle to achieve their own goals. For that reason, the organization must strain for achieving a balance between the particular interests of each group and their common interests (the well-known although rarely respected "*for the best interest of the company*"). As we see, power and the utilization of the different systems of influence are a constant in the majority of the organizations.

As we will see later, the differences related to values, goals, aims and interests, are not something capricious but they belong to the fact that each of the groups has its own vision of the reality and has its own and particular frame of reference. This implies that a fact or circumstance that could be tremendously significant for someone may be irrelevant for "the Other".

Let's talk about perception. Subjectivity is the perception of a same situation from several points of view, generally based on different systems of values. In our opinion, a conflict can be defined as an incompatibility between perceptions, aims and / or emotions between persons and / or groups that claim that the objectives and / or resources are mutually incompatible.

In that situation, in fact, people decide between supporting the discrepancy and supporting the relation, provided that an incompatibility exists between satisfying everybody's needs (or at least part of them) and the sustenance of an affective relation. Supporting the discrepancy generates a cost that we have to be ready to assume.

In practice, there are many occasions where someone is ready to personally assume the cost of supporting this discrepancy but, on the other hand, the organization that person belongs to cannot or doesn't want to allow it.

It is important to never lose of sight the impact that a situation of discrepancy can generate not only in the principal actors of the conflict but also in the people close to them. Further on we will check the mechanics of the so-called "escalation of the conflict" (very often when individuals or groups don't obtain what they need or want, they try their best to obtaining it, involving other persons in the process).

For us, it is necessary to distinguish between a situation of conflict and a problem. A problem refers to a situation, whereas the conflict always refers to relations. This difference is sometimes difficult to grasp due to the fact that, often, when we are immersed in a conflict we use precisely the problem as an excuse.

This aspect seems to us especially relevant: the conflict takes place when an emotional disagreement on policies, processes, activities or outcomes exists between two or more persons. I.e., conflict is, from this point of view, a disagreement between two (or more) parts that feel that they have incompatible aspirations.

When asked to reduce the definition of conflict to the smallest possible number of words, this would be our proposal:

Key sentence

Conflict = incompatible perception of aspirations

Actually, not all the interactions necessarily imply conflict. We believe that, in most interactions, we conduct our relation with "the Others" (whether our current opponents or just plainly the rest of the world) with the appropriate respect and with a positive mindset. Now then, it is most true that any interaction possesses some potential for conflict.

Our position is pragmatic: conflict is going to exist forever. It is something inevitable, like it or not. In spite of our better intentions or despite how hard we try to avoid it, the conflict will appear in our lives and we will find our team, our community and ourselves always on the edge of a potential conflict.

On the other hand, as we will analyze later, conflicts have a peculiarity that it is good to bear in mind: when they appear on the public place what's most likely to happen is that they are already solidly and deeply rooted. For this reason, the detection and the prevention of the conflict in its initial stages is a fundamental aspect for avoiding the consequent escalation.

But before coming to this point, please allow us devote a few lines to analyze a series of popular beliefs that have taken root in our culture (and also in the DNA of many organizations) and that not only don't help us adequately approach and manage the conflict but, moreover, tend to complicate it:

- <u>Dirty laundry is washed at home</u>. I.e., exposing the conflict, putting it under the spotlight ashames us.
- <u>Time cures everything</u>. On the contrary, our experience shows us that what happens is exactly the contrary. Actually, conflict is like a bonfire that always tends to expand.

- <u>In a professional environment we should be capable of coming to agreements</u>. Behind this belief exists the supposition that we all are rational and practical perfect human beings. However the professionals are real persons and they possess a part linked to irrationality, where emotions play a crucial role.
- <u>It is necessary to "negotiate" to solve difficult situations</u>. This belief exercises a powerful influence. Problem: it is not possible to negotiate emotions.
- <u>"People understand each other by **talking** things over"</u>. That's another belief, obviously erroneous. Just have a look around and realize how many people have decided not to talk to each other, think of all the uncountable conflicts that are still pending resolution precisely because of the absence of dialogue or due to the fact that the dialogue has not come to fruition. The belief "People understand each other by **talking** things over" only works if we really know what we are talking about –facts or values for instance– and, besides, if we know how to do it (the talking).

Key sentence

Conflicts can't exist without reasons, be they real or imagined.

Diagnose the Disagreements

If we talk about an organization or a team, it is relatively frequent that the members of a team (or of different teams) are dragged into disagreements (more or less aggressive). When this happens, unfortunately, "the actors" usually don't tend to look for the resolution of the conflict that opposes them.

Quite often, the contend is not obvious in the mind of the actors and what uses to happen is that instead of trading arguments, which would be the most rational thing, they choose to toss those said arguments at each other. For this motive, whenever we face a conflict it is important to formulate three questions for a diagnosis:

- A. What is the nature of the disagreement between the people in conflict?
- B. What are the underlying factors to the disagreement?
- C. What stage of evolution has the conflict reached so far?

A – Nature of the Disagreement

If we consider the first of these three important questions, we will confirm that the nature of the disagreement can evolve according to the questions in contest. We might classify the conflicts into four categories:

1. Conflicts relative to the facts:
Sometimes, the disagreements arise because each person has a different definition for the same problem, because they are in possession of different information, because they accept or reject information relative to the problem, or because their opinion about their own power and authority is not the same.

2. Conflicts relative to the ends:
Sometimes, the disagreement centers on what should be done, on the desirable aims for a department in a company.

3. Conflicts relative to the methods:
Sometimes, people support a different opinion about the procedures, about the strategy or about the tactics best adapted to reach the end desired by all.

4. Conflicts relative to the values.
In other occasions, the disagreement centers on beliefs, on values, on moral grounds, on the underlying opinions relative to what's fair or unfair, right or wrong. This type of conflicts can affect both the election of the ends and of the methods, with the added difficulty of being located in the irrational part of our brains.

Values are a cultural expression of the needs, the basic motivations and the common development requirements to all people. Those needs include safety, identity, recognition and personal development in general. When the basic needs for the survival of a group are unsatisfied, the members of this group tend to fight to satisfy the said needs one way or another. The needs and their satisfaction cannot be negotiated. Nevertheless, as we will comment later, it is possible to identify some ways of satisfying the human basic needs and, in fact, as we will see, the conflict can be approached by means of the process of identification and satisfaction of those said needs.

Beyond the reason why the disagreement takes place, what happens is that the discussions start random shooting, the confusion increases, hence provoking that the parts in conflict don't see with clarity the character of the situation.

Because of that, if we manage to know the source of this difference between people, we will be in a better situation to determine in which way we can orientate the discussion and channel it for the best of the people, the team and the company.

As we will detail later, it will be important to adopt a specific approach when the conflicts have their origin in facts, and some other different approaches when the origin of the conflict resides in the desired ends, and finally adopt some other different approximations if the origin of the conflict lies in methods or values.

B – Underlying factors

Unfortunately, in case of disagreement or conflict between persons it is not sufficient to discover what is the nature of the disagreement. Hence why it is so important to formulate the questions related to the why of the conflict. We propose to consider the following aspects:

- Did all the parts in conflict have access to the same sources of information?
- Did they perceive the common information in a different way?
- How can each of the parts be influenced by their position in the company?

As the reader will see, these questions imply the existence of factors relative to the information about the facts, to the perception and to the role that the involved persons play. For example, the information factors sprout when the different points of view proceed from different information. As a simple metaphor, just have a look at the classical tale of the six blind wise men describing an elephant.

So, when facing a complex problem, if two persons have access to some limited information, it is natural that, at the moment of tackling and solving the problem, they are already in a disagreement about the nature of the above-mentioned problem.

Tale of the six wise blind men and the elephant

Once upon a time in the Antiquity, there were six blind men who spent the daily hours challenging each other trying to decide who was the wisest of them six. To demonstrate their wisdom, they exposed their knowledge in turns and decided who amongst them was the most convincing of all.

Some day, discussing over of the exact shape of an elephant, about which they only new by ear, they could not reach an agreement. Their positions were opposite and as none of them had ever touched an elephant, they decided to venture out in the search of a specimen, in order to clear all doubts.

Walking in a row, with their hands on the shoulders of their predecessors, they initiated their march on a path toward the jungle. They had walked just a while when suddenly they realized that they were close to a large elephant, as they could hint by the sounds it made.

The six wise blind men congratulated. They had been told that elephants used to be gentle animals so no risk was involved.

Finally, they might solve the dilemma and decide what was the real form of the animal.

The first of the blind men, the most determined, rushed to the elephant eager to touch it. Alas, the hurries made him stumble on a twig on the ground and hit the flank of the animal.

– "The elephant – he exclaimed – is like a wall of mud dried by the sun".

The second one of the blind men advanced with more precaution, with his arms widespread. In this position he touched two very long and sharp objects. They were the tusks.

– "The form of this animal is exactly like that of a spear ... undoubtedly it is like that!"

Then the third blind man stepped ahead. The elephant, now curious, wrapped his waist with its trunk. The blind man seized the trunk of the animal and touched it up and down.

– "Listen, the elephant is like a long serpent".

It was the turn of the fourth wise man, which approached from behind and received a soft blow from the tail of the animal. The wise man seized the tail and stroked it up and down.

He did not have any doubts and exclaimed:

– "Now I get it, it is like a old rope".

The fifth of the wise men encountered the ear of the animal and said:

– "None of you is right. The elephant is rather like a large flat leaf".

The sixth wise man was the oldest of them all, and when he walked towards the animal, he did it slowly, bent, resting on a cane. He walked under the belly of the elephant and stumbled over one of its legs.

– "Listen! I am touching it just now and I assure you that the elephant has the form of the trunk of a great palm tree".

They all had experienced by themselves what was the real form of the elephant, and believed that "the Others" were wrong. Satisfied their curiosity, they took the path leading them back home.

Now sitting under their palm tree, they recaptured the discussion on the real form of the elephant; each of them convinced about what was the real form of the elephant.

The factors of perception inevitably enter the scene when two persons construct different images from the same stimuli. Each of us captures and extracts from the information the elements that he, subjectively, considers to be relevant.

Everyone interprets this information in his own way and adds to the raw data a filter made of life experiences that makes him perceive the information through a completely personal filter.

The final image is also personal. It should not be, therefore, surprising that the same fundamental and seemingly not open to discussion "facts" generate, in the mind of different persons, different perceptive pictures.

The "assignment" factors also exercise their influence provided that everyone in the community or in the company occupies a determined position; i.e., enjoys a status. This position or this status can "impose" some pressures, so the discussion has to see with the role that people in conflict play.

Some of our colleagues indicate that (in agreement with the theory of social identity) in a company it is not even necessary for a conflict of interests to exist in order for discrimination to take place between groups. The mere splitting of persons into separated groups drives to favoritism towards people of our own group and to the ostracism of those persons that don't belong. We all have heard of people talking about other departments as "them" vs "we", when we actually all belong to the same company.

Because of that, we always stress the importance of being conscious that the organization is not shaped by a uniform and homogeneous culture but, rather, by multiple subcultures that merely reproduce different styles and visions when facing and understanding reality.

Maybe for that, over the last years many companies have been insisting on the need to building a shared vision of interests and meanings that minimizes great part of the potential conflicts between groups and / or departments. Here, the managers play a critical role: they in the end are the people in charge of developing a common and cooperative spirit towards the fulfillment of shared aims.

In many occasions, nevertheless, a lot of managers practice a type of supervision that causes problems in the work environment, and, consistently, constitute a potential source of subsequent conflicts. Let's think about the impact of the following elements and on the impact of managing them adequately (or not):

- Poor communication
- Popping-up surprises
- Difficulty to understand the reason behind the decisions.
- Development of rumors
- Involved resources
- Disagreement with the person that does things.
- Tension because of the lack of resources or because of the inadequate use of them.
- Conflict of values and actions
- Quite often we dislike in others what we dislike in us.
- When we get stuck in our mindset.
- Leadership problems
- Inconsistency in people' management
- Lack of leadership
- Inflexibility

In any case, knowing why the conflicts appear turns out to be fundamental. Also it is most true that this identification can turn out to be tremendously difficult. The origin of the conflicts can be veiled, especially in those cases where the emotions in play are intense and strong negative feelings exist. As well, multiple triggers can exist, which makes isolating a single reason even more difficult.

The four stages of the conflict

Generally speaking, there is no such conflict that pops up out of nowhere. They all go through a series of stages. The way the energy of the protagonists can be effectively funneled depends on, to some extent, at which stage of the conflict may intervene an outsider (for example, the team leader).

One of the ways to identify the conflict consists of determining in which of its development stages the conflict has entered the public space. As well, this understanding provides good indications over what might happen in the future. These are the stages of the conflict:
- 1.Latent conflict (potential conflict)
- 2.Conflict perceived (realization of the latter)
- 3.Conflict felt (personalization of the conflict)
- 4.Conflict expressed (fights between groups and persons)

Stage 1: The latent conflict

At this stage they are a series of problematic conditions that potentially favor the presence of conflicts. Formally, we should say that conflict doesn't exist yet although it might appear at any moment.

These conditions can be quite diverse: a deficient or ineffective communication, some errors in the formal structure of the organization or the team, like for instance the lack of clarity in the different areas of responsibility, in the levels of authority, in the degree of dependence, etc., As well, the personality of some member of the team can be disturbing for the rest of the bunch. A sarcastic laugh, a grating voice, a despotic attitude, the over-domineering character of a person, an anxious or furious temper, etc.

The idea we want to transmit here is that, quite often, the conditions for the conflict are present, but the parts don't notice it or don't use an adequate strategy to tackle it.

This is, therefore, clearly a situation of latent conflict. And people alien to this situation cannot realize that a conflict actually exists until the parts initiate hostile actions against each other.

This distinction helps us explain why it often seems that the conflicts "arise from the void". Actually, as we say, it never happens that way. Most likely, the conditions have been present way before the hostilities opened up.

Therefore, the perception that the parts have of the existing conditions can reinforce or reduce the probability of a conflict.

STAGE 2: THE PERCEIVED CONFLICT

The perceptive processes can whether create conflicts or avoid them. Feelings and attitudes constitute the most important element in the development of a conflict, or in the fruitful quest for a solution. Probably, the personal personalities play an important role when reacting that way or another, but we are sure that some developed skills may also play a transcendental part.

In this stage, we start perceiving or "feeling" a situation of conflict. There is some awareness of the presence of some conditions that can make the conflict arise. A conflict "is felt" when people put their emotions into play and that creates anxiety, tension, frustration or hostility. In this stage we are finally aware.

When the conflict involves feelings and becomes personal, then it turns into a "felt conflict" (the following stage). As we have already mentioned, in this situation, the degree of confidence between the parts determines the outcome of a potentially troubled situation.

As we will see, the rational and cognitive components of an interaction are – actually – transcendent, but from our point of view what really marks the development of the conflict is the emotions that are put into play.

Stage 3: The conflict "felt"

In this stage, one or both parts take the decision to act. Many conflicts worsen because one of the parts attributes to "the Other" some shady intentions (in general, different from those that "the Other" actually has). This stage is also known as "personalization of the conflict"

Stage 4: The expressed conflict

The leap from a latent conflict to an expressed conflict is marked by a process of escalation, where we see, amongst others, an increase in the number and the magnitude of the topics in dispute, a decrease of the mutual confidence, the utilization of coercive tactics and the polarization of the demands or aims that are pursued.

When this happens, the latent conflict stops being such and turns itself into a manifest conflict. In the majority of occasions, as we indicate, it is extremely difficult to determine and to foresee such a transition.

In this stage the conflict becomes visible through the behavior of the contending parts. This behavior uses to include statements, actions and reactions from the parts in conflict. Those behaviors are the unequivocal materialization of the intentions of the parties, although they often differ from the latter as a result of misunderstandings in the intentions of the interlocutor, or due to the fact that the original intentions get distorted when transformed into concrete behaviors. It is a stage where a real struggle between persons (and, often also between teams) takes place.

Derivative from this situation, there are some consequences that ensue from the interaction action – reaction between the parts in conflict. The mentioned process of escalation is characterized by:

- Increase of the number and the magnitude of topics in dispute
- Increase of the hostility
- Increase of the competitiveness
- Pursuit of extreme –and unrealistic– aims
- Transition from specific problems to general problems
- Increase of the utilization of coercive tactics
- Decrease of the mutual confidence

As we have seen, the results can be functional if the conflict has been adequately managed in its initial stages. The consequence of this process is that the conflict will be productive. Sometimes, nevertheless, the results of the conflict are dysfunctional and have a high impact not only on people that are in direct conflict but also on all those close to them, and by extension, on the groups to which they belong.

Luckily, however, there are some indicators that should alert us of the existence of a latent conflict:

- The corporal language (positions, tone of the voice, volume...)
- The increase in the number of disagreements, whatever the matter
- The unexpected surprises
- Public strong declarations
- The increase in the number of lacks of respect

- The open opposition
- The absence of specific goals
- The non discussion of the progress

The existence of one or several of the mentioned elements can reflect the existence of a conflict and give us hints about the stage of the process we are currently in.

We have often verified that, in many companies and teams, we tend to ignore the existence of a latent conflict and we accept as carved in stone the positive adamant statement: "*in our team we don't have any conflict*".

An important aspect of the conceptual distinction between latent and manifest conflict resides in being able to predict and manage the popping up of situations that could potentially produce irreparable damages to people, to the team and to the company.

A particularity to bear in mind is that, by contraposition, the conflicts that have burst out violently can step back again into latent conflicts, especially when the parts have come to a point of exhaustion. It is not an infrequent process.

Nevertheless, until the underlying conditions of the conflict are analyzed, the conflict will remain latent and without any resolution. In consequence, always will persist the risk that the conflict may show up in a future. When the deep-rooted conflicts are still in their latent phase, it is a good moment to realizing activities of prevention and initiating efforts seeking for better understanding.

Sources of conflict (detail)

- Subjectivity of the perception.
- Trend to see as a personal attack any discrepancy with the facts or with the situations.
- Incomplete information.
- Poor styles of communication (absence of communication, lack of feedback, etc.).
- Disproportion between the needs of the people and those of the groups / companies.
- Difference of interests (including socio-economic and cultural aspects).
- Difference between characters and personalities.
- Pressures that cause frustration.
- Separatisms and divisions.
- Excessive intimacy and excessive interdependence.
- Search of power.
- Dissatisfaction about the supervision styles.
- Poor leadership.
- Lack of openness.
- Leader›s change.

Any of the mentioned reasons may give place to the inception of a conflict.

THE INFERENCE LADDER

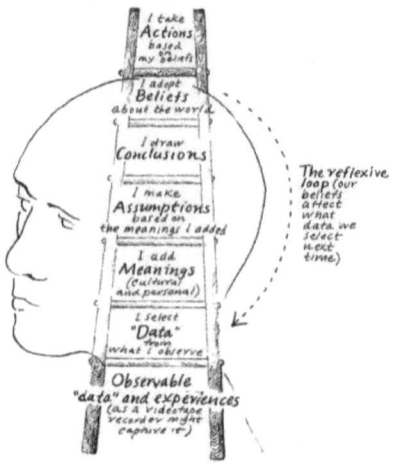

Here before we move any further, we must talk about a very useful concept we will be referring to from time to time, the ladder of inference.

What do we do when we face the events of life? Actually, we do many things we are fully conscious of, but we also do many other things we are not that conscious of and that tend to complicate things and have a very strong impact on the involved interpersonal relations.

When facing a fact, the first thing we all do is filter data. We, as we have said before, interpret the facts on the basis of our beliefs, suppositions, mental models, etc. Most of them are not transparent, i.e., we cannot see them.

These interpretations of "reality" (what is reality?) shape our opinions or judgments about that said information, and those opinions end up constituting "the truth".

The consequence of this process is that we come to conclusions, to decisions for action and to actions that may have no point of contact with the initial fact, thus hampering our relations and even our public image.

This process is what the psychologist Chris Argyris called "the ladder of inference", although generally, it is not a ladder, it a high-speed elevator: something happens and suddenly we are propelled into action.

An example of this ladder might be reflected in the following inferences:

Step 1: " William, my boss, did not comply with a promise he made me".
Step 2: " He is making mistakes".
Step 3: " He is not interested in people".
Step 4: " I believe they should sack him".

Let's see another example:
Step 1: " they said they would invite me to the meeting but they didn't".
Step 2: " they have cheated me".
Step 3: " they don't have integrity".
Step 4: " I will never accept one of their invitations".

How much time do we need to move from step 1 to 4? Very little time actually. The inferences ladder works in the following way from top to bottom (see attached figure):

- I adopt actions based on my beliefs
- I adopt beliefs about the world
- I extract conclusions

- I realize assumptions based on the meanings I add
- I add meanings
- I select information
- I observe information and experiences

Key sentence

> "The mental models are the images, assumptions and stories that we store in our mind about ourselves, about other people, about other companies and about every aspect of the world"

> "As a colored glass pane subtly distorts our vision, the mental models determine what we see"

Peter Senge

How can we avoid smashing our head against the roof at the top of this ladder? In other words, what can we do to adequately manage those inferences?

The answer is easy to utter: admitting that this process exists, beyond that we perceive it or not. Let's want it or not, we human beings tend to pick the data that resonates with our beliefs.

As our beliefs become increasingly rigid throughout the years, the information relevant to us constitutes an ever-shrinking part of reality. When we understand the inferences ladder model (both our own as others'), it is possible to start detecting the incongruities between experience and real information and between actual experience and the information derived from our beliefs.

In our opinion, the ladder of inference is of great usefulness to help us realize that we have leaped several steps to come to a wished conclusion. Because of that, it constitutes a fundamental tool to avoid the escalation of the conflict.

As we will analyze later, when we people don't agree on a conclusion, what we have to do to move forward is explicit both the information we have selected and the steps of our interpretation process. I.e., presenting our ideas and our opinions with a clear language, putting forward the information upon which we elaborate, exposing to "the Others" our rationale, explaining our aim or worry, presenting an offer for action and, finally, checking whether our interlocutor understands what we are currently saying.

Both conflicts solving and rebuilding of interpersonal relations, as well as the search of an effective communication are to a great extent going to depend on this process.

In other words, it is about making our thinking process visible:

- Present the assumptions and the information that define our process
- Explain our assumptions
- Make our rationale explicit
- Explain the context and give examples
- Encourage "the Others" to explore our point of view
- Invite to improvement
- Listen and stay open

LEVELS OF CONFLICT

With the purpose of exhaustively understanding the conflict, we think it is relevant to be conscious of the fact that there are four levels of conflict that are intimately interrelated:

- A – Intrapersonal
- B – Interpersonal
- C – Intragroup
- D – Intergroup

A – INTRAPERSONAL CONFLICT

At this level, the conflict takes place within us. The triggers to this type of conflict can be varied:

- Firm beliefs
- Values
- Ideas
- Predispositions ("I am an optimistic")
- Need for safety
- Some personality traits

It is important to highlight that this type of conflict:
- Provokes strong emotions

- Often, those emotions block us and prevent us from behaving effectively.

What steps can we follow to remain effective most of the time? Putting it in another form, what are the stages to starting being effective?

B – Interpersonal conflict

This type of conflicts takes place between two or more persons that are in opposition (it can be between a boss and a collaborator, two colleagues, a father and son, etc.)

Later on we will present some other specific suggestions to approach this type of conflicts (actually, the present book focus mainly on this typology of conflicts). Nevertheless, here are some ideas that keep a narrow relation with the inferences ladder and with its management:

Stages of the process

"Where am I now? "– "What has happened?"

"How can I be more conscious of it?"

"What does this tells me? How does it fit in what I already know?

"And now what? What changes do I need to adopt?"

"How will I evaluate or check the impact of those changes?"

Discover the thoughts of "the Others":
- Step down our interlocutors ladders
- Use a non-aggressive language

- Extract the underlying rationale
- Request examples
- Verify the understanding of what we have listened to
- Listen and be open

C – Intragroup conflict

This type of conflicts appears within a small group (a department in a company, a family, a school class, etc.). Here the transcendent thing will be to know how the conflict affects the capacity of the group to solve it and, at the same time, how it affects the will of fighting for reaching the goals.

D – Intergroup conflict

The last level of the conflict is the most complicated, probably due to the great quantity of persons involved and the multiple possible interactions between them. Here the conflicts are between families, between employers and unions, between nations, etc. In practice, a conflict may appear at the same time within a group but also between groups. This circumstance does that the analysis of the situation and the eventual strategies of confrontation in this type of conflict use to be complex.

In any case, remember, dear reader, that independently of the level of analysis of the conflict, any conflict possesses some similar characteristics:

- They imply a divergent perception of interests (be it divergent or not in reality). This aspect is important, provided that, as we have seen, it is very habitual that

the involved parts perceive the problem between them in a distorted way.
- There are a limited number of strategies to tackle it. Later on we will present the different methods that we may use to face the conflict.
- They contain a mixture of motives. Especially, as we will see, this happens in those conflicts that are characterized by a high interdependence.
- They may end through a change in attitudes. Any conflict may potentially end with an agreement or a resolution. The agreement implies a behavior change, which takes place when both parts find a way to come to an agreement although their positions remains basically unaltered. The resolution involves as much a modification in the behavior as a mutual attitude change that leads both parts to internalize a new interaction pattern. Obviously, in the latter case, it is very improbable that what originally caused the conflict rises again.
- It produces some results (from innovation to sheer destruction). Not every conflict is, far from it, destructive. As we will see in a few pages, many conflicts are constructive and even desirable.
- It arises from a wide variety of precedents. These previous conditions often predict in a trustworthy enough way the consequence that will have the conflict, and, as well, its sheer development.

Is conflict bad?

In the abundant existing literature on conflicts, the response to this question comes to a great extent determined by the theoretical orientation adopted by the author. This way, there is a traditional vision on conflicts, nowadays partially obsolete, that proclaims that the conflict must be avoided at any cost.

It is most likely that you reader has sometimes heard phrases like these:

- "The conflict destroys the relations. It is safer to ignore the conflict"
- "Normally it is impossible to solve a conflict"
- "I have many conflicts. I am not a good person"
- "There is always someone who ends up hurt in a conflict. If I "lose" I will be deemed as weak and vulnerable"
- "It is a bad idea to have an opinion different from people who are in charge"

A different approach, on the other hand, called "human relations vision", indicates that the conflict is something natural and inevitable in any human group. A third vision, the so-called interactionist, postulates that the conflict can constitute a positive force and may even turn out to be absolutely necessary to achieving the adequate performance of people, teams and companies.

We see therefore that the conflict can undoubtedly be negative and destructive, but it can also be desirable and even necessary from other points of view. Let's examine some aspects of both perspectives:

NEGATIVE ASPECTS OF THE CONFLICT

- It constitutes a potential source of violence.
- It evolves toward hostility and destructive feelings against the one who is perceived as the source of the conflict.
- It is a motive of anxiety, of oppression and of worries that originate psychosomatic reactions (migraines, lumbagos, etc.)
- It is an impulse of activity, to defend our personal position, which can lead to antagonism.
- It originates impotence, poor performance, and inhibits and blocks the person.
- It drives to the formation of groups and of antagonistic blocks (it is not, actually, infrequent that the conflicts between groups tend to become institutionalized)

In a company the conflict is negative when:

- It undermines the common aims
- It reduces the cooperation
- It ends in an inappropriate behavior, in chaos and in confusion
- It divides and separates people
- It reduces the logical actions and increases the emotional behavior

Costs of the conflict

- It destroys the professional relations
- It creates barriers to the individual and organizational efficiency
- It messes up the teamwork
- It creates enemies and secret agendas
- It adds stress to the workplace
- It generates waste of time, resources or money
- It affects the ability of remaining competitive

The conflict can be constructive when ...

- It clarifies the problems and the controversies.
- It helps us solve problems.
- It involves people to solve controversies.
- It provokes an authentic communication.
- It helps us liberate emotions, anxiety and tensions.
- It develops cooperation and the desire to learn.
- It helps develop understanding and skills.
- It promotes growth and efficiency
- It encourages adaptability
- It promotes creativity

In line with the above, for us, the interpersonal conflict is not necessarily bad or destructive. Conflict, as we already said in a couple of occasions, is plainly inevitable. Different persons will have different points of view, ideas and opinions. The fundamental matter, for us, is about how are managed or handled those differences.

Therefore, we can point out that conflict can be contemplated as something dysfunctional and extremely destructive but there are also numerous conflicts that are functional and, therefore, highly constructive. In other words, the functional conflict serves the interests of the company whereas the dysfunctional conflict threatens those very interests.

Actually, in no few cases, interpersonal differences, competition, rivalry and other forms of conflict possess a positive value for the participants and contribute to the efficiency of the social system where they arise.

Hence a moderate level of interpersonal conflict, as we say, can have, between others, the following constructive consequences:

- Increase the available motivation and the energy for the tasks requested by the team or by the company.
- Increase the capacity of innovation of people and of the team / organization.
- Acquisition of a better comprehension of our own position provided that the conflict forces us express our points of view and the arguments upon which they rely.
- Every part can achieve a major conscience of his personal identity.

As we say, what is really interesting is to facilitate a more effective management of the conflict in order to reach one of the two following goals:

- A solution, so that the differences or the original feelings of opposition disappear.
- A control, so that the negative consequences diminish in spite of the fact that, as a minor evil, the opposed preferences and the antagonisms might persist.

In spite of the above-mentioned, we all know that most people adopt openly counter-productive behaviors at the moment of facing a conflict. Later on we will talk with major profusion and detail about it. In general, it is because those persons use to live through the conflict as something negative. Between the behaviors we can see:

1.Ignoring or avoiding the conflicts: The appearance of conflicts provokes that some persons suppress their emotional reactions and look for other ways, even leaving them a troubled situation, and merely pass. The root of this behavior comes determined by not knowing how to approach the problem or by not possessing sufficient skills to adequately negotiate.

Maybe you personally have lived this situation. Ignoring the conflicts, nevertheless, may drive to:

- a.Indignation and resentment
- b.To perpetuate the "we always did it that way"
- c.To drown down new ideas

2.Procrastinating: This behavior is not leading us anywhere, and quite often it can even aggravate the problem as if an interpersonal conflict exists without resolution, there's a high probability that it will continue producing personal frets.

3.Answering aggressively: Here let's be adamant. The one who acts this way is more insecure than he wishes to pretend and he doesn't possess the sufficient skills to solve his problems without appealing to aggressiveness.

Remember, therefore, to conclude this chapter, that the conflicts are inevitable (in the organizations, at home, at school, in the neighbors' community...). Don't think that conflicts are always negative: managed with efficiency they may constitute an opportunity for growth. The key thing is managing them adequately...

Key sentence

"Conflict is neither good nor bad, it is just an integral part of life and is necessary for growth and change"

Maire To. Dugan, "A nested theory of conflict"

Conflict and performance

The tension degree in a conflict is an element to be seriously taken into account. According to the degree, it might be convenient to stimulate the conflict in order to improve performance.

We can distinguish three tension levels in a conflict (low, moderate and high), which have different effects on the utilization of information and on the results of the process of conflict management. The conflicts that present a low level of tension (A) use to lead the parts to stagnation and even to avoidance. We, in this case, don't perceive the sensation of urgency and tend to leave aside information that leads us to stagnation and to poor results.

When in a conflict a moderate level of tension exists (B), the parts seek more information and strain for integrating it. Then we have a larger number of options in mind and, in general, we may find a major motivation for improving the situation.

Finally, in those conflicts with a very high level of tension (C), the involved persons tend to reduce their aptitude to process and evaluate the information. In this context, interrelationships loaded with aggressiveness take place and, as a consequence the relations between people can be seriously damaged. The latter stage is the closest to a destructive conflict.

Actually, the previous record of relation between people involved in the conflict plays a transcendental role in the tension level. We don't have the same starting point if in the past warm relations between the parts have prevailed or if, on the opposite, serious conflicts have taken place between those persons.

As a summary, we can indicate that those conflicts with a very high or very low intensity use to damage more than benefit the parts. On the other hand, moderate conflicts tend to be of benefit to the parts.

CONFLICT AND PERFORMANCE ORGANIZATIONAL

Situation	Level of conflict	Type of conflict	Organizational characteristics	Level
A	Low or null	Dysfunctional	Apathetic, static, doesn't respond to the change, lacking ideas	Low
B	Ideal	Functional	Viable, self-critical, innovative	High
C	High	Dysfunctional	Upset, chaotic, non-cooperative	Low

THE DRAMATIC TRIANGLE

The conflicts so-called "of relation" can be understood much better if we analyze them relying on a simple and, at the same time, tremendously useful model: the so-called "dramatic triangle".

According to a famous investigator, Stephen Karpman, in conflicts people tend to use some patterns of interpersonal communication. Those patterns, in his opinion, are absolutely predictable (before the development of a conflict we all have heard something like: " *I knew that this would end this way*").

The same patterns are used in posterior interactions (with a hidden agenda) and drive to the collapse of the communication process and, inevitably, to the increase of interpersonal problems and negative feelings.

As you may hint, understanding those psychological games constitutes the first step to put them to an end, and from then on, look for the options best adapted to adequately relate to "the Others"

Why do we play those games when they are essentially negative?

Basically because we all repeat models from the past, i.e., behaviors that soothe us, provided that, for us, they are well known. Actually, in those specific moments, we are not fully conscious of the mechanism we are using, and we ignore that a different way of acting may exist. In fact, what those behaviors provoke is reaffirm our beliefs and our position (remember why the inferences ladder appears). In other words, those behaviors tend to self-feedback.

And hence we avoid other approaches to the question.

Consequently, all of us, from childhood, learn to relate to the world that surrounds us and obtain what we need or what we wish through a series of roles that, essentially, have a strong cultural component.

Those roles have two facets: an internal one (they are a part of our interior dialogue), but also an external one (we adopt those roles when relating to "the Others").

Did you notice, for instance, that with some people arguments always end up the same way? raising their voice, with disappointment, nastiness, anxiety ... This type of repetitive situation leaves us with the feeling that it is not possible to change anything, it is what in this context is named "psychological games".

Karpman, as we say, has simplified and systematized all those "games" into a model easy to understand, observing that it implies three possible functions: a persecutor, a savior-or rescuer and a victim.

Let's think for a moment about a teenager that has to do his homework: his "persecutor" tells him that he must do it and makes him feel bad if he doesn't study; his "victim" makes him feel unfortunate, he may think that despite studying hard he will not pass or that he always have to do boring things; his "savior" may tell him that he will study later, or that if he doesn't make the grade, well that won't matter that much.

It is necessary to suppose that as we mature, we learn to motivate ourselves. We learn how to be ourselves and to relate to "the Others" without assuming learned or faked roles. Interaction and interior dialogue are based on other principles: to negotiate and to reach satisfactory agreements (to be orientated to aims), to be honest and to be in disposition of assuming challenges although we don't always meet them, and to respect "the Others" and ourselves. But, obviously, this is only a supposition.

Those roles, as we say, are ingrained in us since infancy and are so deep-rooted that, in some occasions, they sabotage our relational life as adults and make us spiral down into a vicious and very unsatisfactory circle.

In fact, Karpman affirms that those roles are carved into our behavioral "closet" and that it is very difficult to step away from them.

The manifested conflicts are the result of latent processes where the involved persons adopt in a semi-unconscious form some not very legitimate roles from "the Other's" point of view. Consistently so, they feel aggrieved for what "the Others" do to them, but they don't take responsibility for the damage that they might be causing (or they justify it because of the damage they have previously suffered). Hereby, they see themselves as the victims of the situation and perceive "the Other" as the only culprit of the situation created. As the reader can imagine, the result of this process is an escalade of mutual hostilities.

When analyzing any troubled situation, it is good to pay attention to the roles that people in conflict adopt and how they move to and fro between the three roles: " the savior", "the" victim, "the persecutor". Practically all the conflicts include these internal dynamics, although with different degrees of intensity. In some occasions, a conflict can last very little and practically not leave any sequels. Other conflicts, on the other hand, can last a lot of time and may make the involved persons suffer a lot. And yes, unfortunately, many conflicts can also have disastrous consequences.

Because of that, Karpman indicates that those roles develop a tragic triangle as in his opinion; in general, each of those roles frequently finishes feeling frustrated, angry and embittered, and thus embittering the life of "the Others".

Let's see in more detail the three positions through which we walk through in a process of conflict with "the Others".

THE PERSECUTOR (ATTACKING)

Attacking is taking advantage of the weaknesses of "the Other" so we discharge our internal anger. Attacking is acting so "the Other" feels guilty, humiliated and scared. Persecution is an act of revenge and of vanity. The one who attacks abuses of his power and is driven by his hostile feelings.

Actually, it is very difficult to admit that someone is being controlled by his vindictive desires or simply that his purpose is to give free rein to his accumulated anger. Hence it is so easy to self-deceive with such rationalizations as *"He started it all"* or *"he deserves to be punished"*.

Beyond the fact that these comments might contain some truth, it is true that to "the persecutor" this situation is fine, as he can give free rein to his resentments. In the same way, and that's the bottom line, he takes advantage of the situation as he sees that his opponent is in a weak moment and cannot defend himself.

When someone assumes the role of "persecutor" he conveys, although not in a verbal way, a message similar to: " *I am the good guy and you are the villain. I'm gunning for you"*.

In this role we experience contained anger, contempt and a wish to damage (by words or by acts).

THE SAVIOR

Many conflicts explode because someone, given the moment, could not erect the proper firewalls and, with the purpose of pleasing "the Other" or just for being useful, overprotected "the Others" making possible that way that they become increasingly demanding or ungrateful.

Saving implies offering help. Nevertheless, this is neither healthy nor opportune. Then why is this behavior expressed? Because by acting so we can build a self-image of kindness and care.

It is not easy at all to admit that behind many "disinterested" helps exists a need to see ourselves deemed as necessary and to experience a high level of pride and of self-complacency. Always remember that the adoption of those roles is almost always realized in an unconscious way.

Nevertheless, it is possible to perceive that a salvation -instead of a genuine help– has happened because the "savior", sooner or later will attack the very one he saved. Actually, whereas the genuine help is provided generously and serves to increase the resources of the person who has been helped (somehow, we teach that person "how to fish"), salvation implies that the helped person is more dependent on external help and becomes more demanding in relation to the savior (in other words, sooner or later he asks for "more fishes").

When helping and caring about "the Other's, the "savior" is transmitting in a non-verbal way a message like this: "*I feel fine helping you, you feel bad if you need my help*". Or this other message: "*With me being around you don't have to worry about anything, I will do it for you*". Or this one. "*What would be of you without me*".

When someone places himself in the position of "savior", he experiences a great worry for "the Other", he anticipates his needs, he insists on helping, advising and orientating. That person feels very happy seeing that the "the Others" need him and that they are grateful for his efforts. In spite of the fact that sometimes he notices that something is not OK or that he starts getting tired of this role, the "savior" continues straining and eventually starts thinking that "the Others" are selfish and ungrateful.

The victim

The same way as when someone meets difficulties he can adopt the victim's role, also he may resort to this role when being stalked or saved.

The person who sees himself as a victim doesn't feel responsible neither for giving a response to the challenges he is finding on his path nor for modifying the attitude that he is adopting before those circumstances.

When someone adopts the role of "savior", the "victim" accepts that overprotection and then self-annuls. As a consequence of it he sees himself unable to put into play or develop the resources required to tackle the problem.

If he stands before a "persecutor", the "victim" feels sorry, feels small and strives to find "saviors" to take revenge on his behalf. The one who feels a victim thinks it is right to counterattack and exert revenge.

The person that feels a "victim" feels sorry about his bad luck and succumbs to discouragement and eventually suffers. Provided that the unexpected and misfortunes alter their emotions, those persons need time and support to overcome their pain. Unconsciously, the victim basks in his own pain and rejoices at it. It is difficult to concur with it, but below the apparent weakness of the person that plays the role of "victim" predominates a feeling of anger and, precisely because of that, eventually the "victim" ends up persecuting someone.

Actually, it is quite frequent that the "victim", in a given moment, feels unsatisfied. He can be bored or, simply, demands more attention. Here the drama begins with a change of role. The victim turns into a persecutor, into an aggressor, normally without any apparent motive or for just a seemingly apparent trifle. He does it without leaving his victim's role. He then appears as a victim when actually he is a persecutor.

Among the advantages of being a victim we can find:

1. – Avoiding responsibility

Provided that the person feels bad, because of a particular situation in his life, he justifies why he is inactive, sad and embittered. A victim feels that he cannot be forced to stick to his commitments because of: *"can't you see how I am feeling?"*.

2. -Having an occupation

A victim centers on his misfortune and focus on his discomfort all the time.

3. – Having a vector for intimacy and social contact

In front of misfortune, people who adopt the role of "victims" always have some topics to talk about. This facilitates intimacy and in turn supplies the raw material for their inner group of friends or colleagues to talk about them; (better criticized than ignored).

4. -Attracting persons that play complementary roles

The victim is at the mercy of a sadistic persecutor who systematically scourges and humiliates him. Eventually, then appears the rescuer (the savior), who saves, at least temporarily, the victim from the aggression.

The weird thing is that the victim rarely ends up being saved because he strongly sticks to his condition and, sooner or later, returns to it. Besides, roles may swap and suddenly the victim assumes the persecutor's position and accuses the savior of something like: *"Look what happened by your fault"*; or the persecutor turns into a victim.

5. -Manipulating and even extorting his people

A victim feels entitled to give orders, to accuse, to demand. If people don't notice him *"he feels bad, very bad"*, and also makes people that surround him feel bad.

6. -Attacking in a passive-aggressive way figures of authority, including your own savior

As an extension of the previous point, a victim may puzzle even the mightiest and drag the dynamics towards his "own playfield".

It is good to remember again that sticking to the victim role is typically an unconscious mechanism and precisely it is why it is that strong. Obviously, people don't easily admit that they have entrenched in this victim's position.

The person that adopts the role of "victim" transmits a non-verbal message that says: "*isn't that terrible what happens to me?*" Or "*how poor of me!*".

The paradoxical thing is that a well-balanced and emotionally stable person will not accept anybody rescuing him, among other reasons, because he is perfectly capable of identifying and solving his problems.

It is because of that, as Karpman understood, that we end up rescuing victims that accept being rescued, without realizing they are reinforcing our rescuing instincts and behaviors.

The victims are actually capable of taking care of them, although neither they nor we will admit it. Generally, our victims are situated in one of the corners of the triangle, hoping that other persons walk the first step and dive into the triangle with them.

Then, those persons are ruled by their need of being reaffirmed in that behavior. Frequently they end up narrowly tied to this type of persons, which ends up leading them without remedy to emotional destruction if they don't adopt proactive measures.

The attempt to control and direct them provokes that they remain under their thumb. The controller is now being controlled. And if being controlled by someone is a bad thing, it is even worse being controlled by someone with the above-described characteristics.

WHO'S THE CULPRIT?

When a conflict appears we tend to focus on the eternal problem of the responsibility or guilt. Again and again, we try to determine who's the culprit (generally, actually, we tend to decide it is the opposite party), instead of thinking about the role that we play in the conflict (i.e. our responsibility) or even in thinking about the problem itself.

The responsibility in front of a conflict, in many occasions can be debatable. "I would not have done this or said that, ...", etc.

When we come to pointing at culprits, we put all our determination and go to great lengths to remain free of guilt and to identify who has been the real culprit of the conflict. Nevertheless, not always can we find an indisputable culprit, or affirm that a given person should be entirely guilty of a problem. In some cases, the guilt uses to be split between the people involved in the problem, as the latter may be pretty ambiguous.

But, beyond looking for a culprit, what we lose of sight is that what really matters is the essence of the problem or of the conflict itself. If instead of centering on the possible or supposed culprit of the problem (my boss, my colleague, my item or my parents), we would focus on the real problem ("*I am being psychologically harassed*") then we would have more possibilities of beginning to solving the problem.

Often, we ear things like: " *My boss yells at me, in spite of the fact that I do my job. He is very inconsiderate. I try to explain things to him, but he doesn't listen to me*", or also, things like: " *My partner lies to me, he promises he will change, but he always misbehaves again, even when I forgive him and attempt to make him understand that he is misled*" ...

In these examples, it is good to observe how the emphasis is not placed on the problem, but always on the "culprit" to our penuries.

Actually, the victims of emotional abuse (or of psychological harassment) are not the culprits of the improper behaviors of those who ill-treat them, but it is relevant for the victims of those abuses to understand that the emotional bullies who take unfair advantage of them will change only if the victim does something about it.

Returning to the essence of the problem, what's fundamental is, precisely, to understand what the mechanism and the nucleus of the problem are. In the previously mentioned cases, the problem is: " a boss that commits abuse of authority and humiliates an employee" and "a selfish and immature person who cannot adequately function in a couple relation".

When we stop centering our attention on "the culprits" and start analyzing the essence of a problem, its structure, its basis or foundation, it is then when we really begin to understand it and, in consequence, may manage that type of conflict.

It is neither about adopting, therefore, some personal attitude in front of a conflict, nor is it about what the interlocutor does or doesn't, it is about a problem with a clear "name and face". When we start understanding the problem, we can modify our attitude and, hereby, put away the troublemakers that poison our life.

In other words, if we ourselves don't erect healthy barriers, it is not likely that "the Others" will do it, specially when it is about immature persons that tend to knock down the rights of their interlocutors.

For this reason, as we say, it doesn't matter who the culprit is, what really matters is wondering what the real problem is.

For all of those reasons, the vision of the conflict that Karpman proposes seems very interesting.

In our opinion, the value of this model rests on that it can help us acquire conscience of the reasons and secret motivations of apparently "legitimate" and reasonable acts (at least in a situation of conflict). The model also helps us not to fall into self-deception: we can be legitimately angry and, besides, have the desire of attacking. Or we may be helping and "saving" at the same time. Or we can be an adverse circumstances victim and feel ourselves as a "victim".

The best way of avoiding the dramatic triangle is to remain in a state of Adult. In other words, persecution, salvation and psychological crybaby are obviously symptoms of immaturity. Because of it, taking conscience of those states (realizing what we are playing at) makes possible the spontaneous appearance of healthier and more effective forms of confronting relations and conflicts.

The real alternative to the dramatic triangle consists then of taking conscience of the existence of these psychological games and react when these trends show up in us.

From another perspective, you can imagine what acting from out of the triangle supposes and take conscience of those moments where instead of acting out of anger, pain or pity we adopt more effective and wiser strategies.

What are then those strategies? Fundamentally three:

1 – Instead of attacking, we establish limits and protect ourselves

We mean here to clearly and calmly express what we cannot stand. For that, we must be able of canalizing our anger before acting. In some cases, as we will see, this can imply waiting for our temper to abate before taking any course of action.

We express our anger with words, we put forward concrete and firm requests and at the same time, in those cases where necessary we interpel our opponent or even we chastise him, making sure —never forget that— that we respect his dignity and avoid abusing of his vulnerability.

2 – Instead of saving, we "open doors"

We make sure ourselves that when helping, we are fomenting that the interlocutor feels really supported when acting on his own, when exploring his own resources and assuming the control of his actions.

In other words, what we are doing is making possible for the interlocutor to grow up and face his personal difficulties.

Obviously, this implies learning how to say "no" to unreasonable or inadequate requests.

As well, it supposes stopping helping when we perceive that we are on the brink of starting attacking.

3 – Instead of being victims, we use our power

We are not entirely responsible for what we have to live through, but what entirely depends on us is the attitude we adopt when facing all those situations that elude our control. When someone decides to adopt an active attitude in front of the difficulties and chooses to use his resources, he begins to experiment and, therefore, to be conscious of his own power to face the most adverse circumstances.

The one who feels a victim attracts persecutors and saviors on equal measure and thus enters a vicious circle (we should more properly use the word "triangle"). Anyone who is capable of taking the helm of his own life, even in difficult moments, always finds some support and thus increases his resources when facing confrontation.

Personal Styles to Confront the Conflict

We tend to respond to troubled situations with a predominant style that blossoms up in a set of concrete behaviors. Although we all have a certain style that uses to be the domineering one in most of the occasions, we possess the aptitude to modify the above-mentioned style if we are conscious of it and if consciously we decide to make a decision, instead of drifting led by our own inertia.

Apparently, it may seem that some styles are more adequate than others, more politically correct, and we can be led into thinking that in consequence we must tend towards them. Nevertheless, if we delve a bit, it is not always like that.

Many conflicts, because of their own nature or due to the characteristics of the situation or of the parties, exclude collaboration, which at first looks like the most desirable thing. In other occasions, a style considered at first sight as negative or as not desirable might be the best adapted as the first response before a conflict.

The model developed by Thomas-Kilmann helps us examine those trends or personal styles that, as we say, we all use at the moment of facing the conflicts.

Actually, the answers we give to interpersonal confrontations tend to form a part of one out of five categories that we mention next.

Those five categories or styles are:

- 1.To impose
- 2.To elude
- 3.To negotiate
- 4.To collaborate
- 5.To yield

Adopting a specific style depends essentially on the response we give to the following question:
What is our real aim?
- To support our personal aims, or
- To support the relation (disposition to cooperate)

1 – Imposition

Imposition, also called domination or confrontation, takes place when one or both parts involved in the conflict try to satisfy his own needs independently of the impact they have on the interlocutor.

When imposition is used as the only way of confronting a conflict it can be assumed that the involved people seek absolute victory. Actually, it is about an aggressive approach without restrictions. This approach can express through behaviors of direct aggression (reproaches, threats, accusations, calumnies, verbal or physical violence, etc.) or through conducts of indirect aggression (active resistance, sabotage, denial of the obvious, etc.)

Nevertheless, as the reader hints at, there are different problems associated with the utilization of this aggressive approach. Besides losing in the specific matters of the conflict, the losing party also sees his self-esteem damaged and can even perceive his social prestige as in jeopardy.

It is obvious that if the interlocutor possesses a power equaling ours, the situation may be different. We talk here about competition. Essentially, it is about the same approach but when there is –or is perceived as such– a similar power, one of the parts decides to answer to the imposition with an imposition in the opposite direction.

It is not difficult to imagine how this situation may end. A struggle starts, a struggle that involves many people and eventually everybody ends up losing something.

Imposition can produce bitter victories, where the winners experience important losses that had not been initially considered (what happens with loyalty? or with commitment? or with the implication of the people that feel they had been coaxed?).

For example, at the workplace, someone can win a dispute through imposition, but this style of confrontation can enormously harm a long-term effective relation and, therefore, destroy the possibility of future effective collaborations with the interlocutor.

Competing implies being conscious of the following thing:

- Probably only the strongest will win (only probably)
- Everyone fights for his own interests
- The effort centers on examining how it is possible to win, or to force "the Other" to give me what I want
- When we compete, what we do is try not to show weaknesses and, at the same time, try to identify the weaknesses of "the Others" and exploit them
- The metaphor of war is the best descriptive about what this style means

Nevertheless, as we were previously saying, this "competing" style can be justified in a series of situations:

- If we have the power, in emergency situations (where a rapid and decisive action is needed).
- In important matters that must find closure in spite of the fact that they are unpopular
- For the better good of the company (and knowing that we are right)
- To protect ourselves against people that try to gain advantage precisely from our non-competitive behavior.

2 – To elude

The second possible approach to tackle the conflict is the one that takes place when one or both parts admit that a conflict exists but, on the other hand, act stepping back from it or procrastinating. This style is called "to elude".

As we can see, it is about a passive approach in front of the conflict, an approach that some people call "don't rock the boat".

The manifestations of this style can be very diverse: postponing the conflict, putting forward excuses, minimizing the problem, using generalizations, etc.

The elusive approach avoids the problem or the situation (because of it some authors call this style "avoidance") and essentially what it does is precisely dodging the harshness of the situation. Some experts distinguish between the short and the long term in the avoidance of the conflict. This way, inaction is a temporary way of not doing anything (actually, in some cases it may be very handy to help us clarify some concepts), whereas retreat is rather a permanent movement to move away from the conflict.

From what we have seen, especially in the business world, this is a style commonly used by managers that don't seem to be emotionally capable of approaching the conflict. Some underlying beliefs to this style are:

- "I prefer not fighting it"
- "It is easier to let things fix by themselves"
- "It is not worth straining"
- "Anyway, it is not important for me"
- "I will obtain what I need another way"

All in all, and as we have insinuated, this style can be effective when the matters are not important and give us a period "of latency".

It is also most true that when this style is used, the conflict may live its own life. I.e., avoiding the conflict may prevent it from further escalating (think about your typical snowball as an illustrative metaphor of the situation).

Beside the already exposed reasons, the "elusive" style can be adequate in situations like:

- When the matter is really trivial or some more important matters exist
- When the potential damage of the confrontation is major than the benefits that stem from its resolution
- When one needs time to calm down, to reduce tensions, to acquire some skills or to recover the composure or the perspective
- When it is necessary to obtain more information
- When other people can solve the conflict more effectively than we can
- When there are few opportunities to satisfy our expectations
- When the matter to deal with seems to be a symptom of some more important matter

3 – To accommodate (submission)

The accommodation takes place when one of the parts solves the conflict surrending to "the Other" at the expense of, at least, some of his own needs. As you may see, it is about a passive approach and, given its particularities, it is also called "smoothing".

Someone can adopt this style out of altruism, thinking that for justice to prevail one has to yield, for the possible achievement of aims (short or medium-term) or simply to avoid the costs associated with the clash with the interlocutor.

Actually, accommodation can be a rational approach if the interlocutor possesses a crushing power and besides has the desire to use this power or, at least, we suppose that this possibility exists. There is another good reason why this approach is useful: if the relation between the parts turns out to be much more important than the matter that has provoked that specific conflict, both parts may be more inclined to look for accommodation.

In this approach, therefore:

- Relation is more important than decision
- Harmony always prevails

Some underlying beliefs of people that choose this style can be:

- *"If I give "the Others what they want, they will later pay me back"*
- *"It is important to be nice to "the Others"*
- *"My needs on this matter are not that important"*

Although this approach could seem to be rather submissive, there are several situations where the approach "accommodating" can be sensible:

- When we realize that we are wrong

- When the matter is more important to the interlocutor than to us
- When we need "to accumulate credit" for other matters that are more important (in another context, this approach is named strategies "of second order")
- When keeping on with the competition would only damage our intentions
- When preserving harmony and avoiding the clash turn out to be specially transcendent
- When, with people under our responsibility, we want to promote the development of our collaborators and decide to allow them learn from their own mistakes

We want to underline here something about this style: although well known by all it is still important: too much adjustment can lead to experiment feelings of rancor, of injustice and of disappointment.

4 – To collaborate

Collaboration is trying that one or both parts completely satisfy the needs of both. With the collaboration both parts can end out winning the conflict. This approach assumes that both parts possess legitimate aims and that creative thinking can transform the conflict into an opportunity so both parts may reach their aims.

The underlying beliefs and the efforts that are realized in this approach are similar to this:

- "We both can obtain what we want"
- "We are together in this endeavor"
- "There is a creative solution that has not yet happened to us"

- "Together we can make it better than we initially thought"
- "What are our common interests?"

This approach is also named "creative conflicts solving" and, as we see, requires that at least one of the parts (preferably the two) sees beyond the problem put forward on the table (actually it works the best when the person and the problem are clearly separated).

Using this approach implies that the parts are ready to openly interchange the information about their priorities or about their preferences, to put their ideas in common, to look for coincidences in their interests, etc.

To attain this, what the parties try to do is what we commonly call "to enlarge the cake" (i.e., to incorporate new elements into the conflict, to add resources, etc.) and to eliminate the elements that interfere in the possibility of reaching a satisfactory agreement and of developing new options.

This proceeding requires imagination and a high degree of cooperation and thus often consumes a great quantity of time and energy. All in all, a collaborative approach before the conflict can lead to two winners and, therefore, contribute to the quality of the personal and labour relations.

There are numerous studies that state that people and companies that insist on the collaboration reach a major percentage of success that those that prefer other ways of solving their conflicts. For this, later on, we will centre with more detail on this approach for conflicts solving.

These are some situations where this specific approach is most suitable:

- When the concerns of both parts are considered to be too important not to be properly tackled
- To find an integrative solution

- When the aim is to put to a test our own assumptions, or to understand better the points of view of "the Other"
- When there is a need to combining people ideas with different perspectives of the problem
- When commitment can thrive if we include the concerns of "the Other" in a consensus decision
- To work on the negative feelings that have been interfering in an interpersonal relation

5 – TO YIELD (OR BETTER PUT "TO BARGAIN" OR "COMPROMISE")

In a strict sense, similar to the French term "compromis", i.e. "an average point". In Spanish, we might replace the word "commitment" with "cesión".

Yielding takes place when the parts involved in the conflict find themselves stuck halfway in the pursuit of their aims. It is about seeking a partial satisfaction to the worries of both parts. As a consequence, the solutions that are sought are those that turn out to be acceptable over those that are ideal. With this approach, nobody wins or loses completely.

Some beliefs and implicit comments in this approach are:

- "We can't both of us obtain what we want"
- "Each one must give away a bit"
- "Let's split the difference"
- "Let's meet halfway"
- "We both need to give and to receive"

In some cultures, this approach is looked at very positively. Nevertheless, this attempt for both parts to be partially satisfied can constitute the primer for future conflicts. One of the evidences that we have observed is that, in environments where people know that this approach is used as an acceptable method for confronting conflicts, people tend to bargain harder than they would done in the first place.

The "yield" approach is also used:

- When the aims are moderately important but the effort is not worth the potential trouble that can provoke the utilization of some more assertive approaches.
- When two opponents with equal power are strongly compromised with mutually exclusive aims (for example, unions and employer)
- When it is necessary to reach temporary agreements in complex matters
- To come to an opportune solution under the pressure of time
- As a fallback style, in case the collaboration or the competition styles fail

The five above-described personal styles for tacking conflicts:
- Provide a structure for the action
- Help us choose a style to manage the conflict
- Increase our understanding of the conflict
- Help us evaluate our own leadership style

As we were initially saying in this chapter, numerous studies have been performed to determine if there is a style that is best suitable when we have to solve a conflict. We have already outlined the response: every style has its advantages and its disadvantages. Depending on the situation, it will be more convenient to apply one strategy or another.

In a managerial environment, for example, the style that you put into play can differ depending on if your interlocutor is a superior, a collaborator or a colleague. Because of our experience in companies, in this situation, one tends to use mainly collaboration when dealing with superiors, bargaining when facing the colleagues (our peers) and, unfortunately, imposition when the interlocutor is a collaborator.

In any case, the aptitude to choose the correct approach constitutes a key skill in the conflicts solving process.

We invite our reader to analyze his predispositions and his trends before the conflict. What is your preponderant style? And in what situations?

Understanding the Conflict

As we were previously saying, a conflict arises when any contraposition of aims, goals or methods of two or more people enters the stage.

The conflicts basically initiate from a perception problem. Because of a particular interpretation of facts or because a dissatisfaction in needs, one of the parts detects a situation that somewhat affects its aims. Remember that the involved parts have to perceive that a conflict exists. Whether the differences are real or not is, in practice, irrelevant. Nevertheless, if there is no conscience of the conflict, then it doesn't exist.

Only in the moment when, at least, a part perceives that "the Other" has affected him negatively (or is on the verge of affecting him), is when the above-commented process of conflict begins.

The expression of a conflict can vary from a subtle act of disagreement to the expression of the most violent opposition. Obviously, a conflict may arise in any area: within a group, a department, a business or even appear as an organizational conflict.

It is true that, normally, there's always an event that ignites it. We can refer to this moment as "the spark": a culminating point where it is possible to admit (sometimes not without effort) that the conflict has exploded. From that moment on, people involved (or, at least one of them) admit that they are in opposition.

In spite of that, it is most true that sometimes it is very difficult to identify the beginning of any conflict. Conflict is always based on a social relation and, therefore, tends to increase or diminish in intensity (according to the evolution of that relation), instead of merely begin and end.

Nevertheless, being aware of the event that provoked the appearance of the conflict turns out to be important, because it indicates the development of the relation and the point where the tensions started soaring. Sometimes the spark and the problem that it unveils are precisely the only aspect that separates both persons and, in consequence, the only matter that it is adamantly necessary to tackle. Nevertheless, in the majority of occasions, this spark or trigger represents only the most visible matter that has led the relation to a clash.

Underneath the particular matter at hand, a series of differences, of misunderstandings and of disagreements are often cloaked and it is necessary to unveil them, as they constitute the basis and the structure of the relation in dispute.

To better understand the conflict and, whenever needed, to intervene in order to regulate it, we have to unveil that ground and to be in disposition to recognize the features typical of the conflict in general.

Power and self-esteem

Any conflict, whatever the level where it takes place, takes its root in two phenomena: power and self-esteem, which in the middle of a conflict, go closely hand in hand. The interpersonal disputes, as we already said, take place from the thinking perception that the interlocutor is the one that prevents and impedes the accomplishment of our desires, our interests or our needs.

It is furthermore about whether we can obtain what we wish. As we have previously mentioned, the conflict explodes when what we want is incompatible with what "the Other" wants or does.

POWER

In the middle of this perceived opposition, power has to see with mutual influence. When analyzing a conflict, it is good to detail the basis and the scope of influence of every intervener. We can mention some basis for influence:

- Economical, educational or social level
- Access to material resources
- Access to the sources of information
- Aptitude to control or to manipulate what "the Other" wishes

Equality or not in influence always concerns directly the process and the very result of the conflict. One of the recommendations that we suggest to follow when intervening in a conflict is precisely of straining for equalizing the imbalance of influences between the parts.

SELF ESTEEM

On the other hand, when we are in opposition with the interlocutor, we tend to inevitably enter personal valuations: *"He has challenged, questioned and confronted me"*.

Almost always we react that way and it is natural that we wonder:
- How will I respond?
- What will "the Other" think?
- Will I retain my dignity?

All we human beings have this type of reaction, and it stimulates us in a clear direction: personalizing the conflict. In other words, what we often do is, in fact, answer to the person who defies us and not to the actual matters that really separate us.

This proceeding always intensifies and polarizes the conflict. The mistake remains when we think that we will uphold our dignity only if we conquer "the Other". Although actually it is not that simple, the only alternative to this situation is to face the conflict without personalizing it and the only way of doing that is through understanding the following:

- The differences of opinion about the procedure to follow
- The differences of values
- Some concrete questions (about money, time, rights, compensation, etc.)

As we will examine later on, the comprehension of a conflict is enormously facilitated if we are capable of separating those different facets.

Concretely, the matters are the different areas of discrepancy or of incompatibility that have to be treated to solve the problem. On the other hand, the interests are the reasons why each of those matters is of real importance for people involved in the conflict. Finally the needs are the minimum necessary needed to satisfy someone, in a tangible or intangible form.

STRUCTURE AND DYNAMICS OF THE CONFLICT

The processes involved in conflicts are complex processes though, once initiated, they use to display some common features. As a whole they form a structure that defines them. This structure consists of the interaction of three elements, the so-called "three Ps":

- People,

- Process,
- Problem (or essential differences).

As we will see, when we analyze any conflict it is important to consider those three aspects.

People

The first task when analyzing a conflict is about understanding the magnitude of the problem. Here, several questions are important:

- Who is involved?
- What is their role?
- How much influence do they possess?

In an interpersonal dispute normally there are only two persons involved. Nevertheless, a conflict at school, in an organization or in a community, almost always involves multiple persons or groups, even though in its origin the problem began only between two persons.

In any case, it is indispensable to determine who is directly involved in the conflict and who, albeit not directly involved, may influence the direction and the result of the process.

Subsequently, it is good to have in mind that each of the persons involved in a conflict possesses some values, interests, needs and a perspective on the situation that motivate their actions.

All this translates in practice into a concrete attitude that this person adopts in relation to the problem, and that represents the solution preferred by him.

Besides, the perspective that this person has formed in accordance with how he was affected by what happened. When someone explains his personal perspective, he always mixes his feelings with the facts. For those of us that intervene in the conflict, this supposes bearing in mind that normally the emotions will dominate over the reason, that everyone will have his own particular perspective of the problem and that, probably, nobody will perceive it in its entirety. From here arises the urgent need to separate the person from the conflict.

As we will see, it doesn't suit to centre specifically on the motives of the people involved in the conflict or on the character of the above-mentioned motives. When intervening in a conflict, we are trying to solve the problem, not to judge, nor to despise people. One of the keys is therefore to know in depth the "mental map" of people involved in the conflict (i.e., how they see and feel).

It is good to stress that, as the number of persons involved in the conflict increases, it becomes more and more difficult to come to an agreement, just because of the existence of more preferences and more expectations that have to be coordinated.

THE PROCESS

The process includes the declared story of the conflict, as well as the involved communication processes, the utilization of the verbal and non-verbal language of the involved actors.

Therefore, when talking about the process there are several aspects or facets that it is necessary to take care of. First it is fundamental to analyze the communication processes. As you may see, the communication tends to deteriorate in parallel with the escalation in the intensity of the conflict: the more intense the conflict, the worse the communication.

This situation takes place because when the problem intensifies, we increasingly make ourselves strong in our position and, as a consequence of it, we tend to listen less to "the Other". It is usual to resort to stereotyping the interlocutor or even to insulting him.

The result of this situation is that we start accusing each other. This way, we tend to look at the past so we can confirm the guilt of "the Other". We don't think in terms of what we can do here and now to ensure the future of the relation, but in terms of inflicting damage on "the Other" and in exposing his guilt.

Another specificity is that when we are immersed in conflicts we almost always look for some people on whom to rely. When we have a problem with someone, we talk about that person instead of talking with. This proceeding accentuates the degradation of information, the appearance of stereotypes, and thus increases the probability of coalitions to appear, thus making the conflict more extreme and, logically, more difficult to manage.

THE PROBLEM

When analyzing the problem, it is necessary to distinguish between the unnecessary conflict and the justifiable conflict. Both form a structure that shapes the dynamics and the structure of the problem. Nevertheless, we will be able to understand the conflict much better if we are capable of distinguishing between them.

The justifiable conflict is based on essential differences, matters and concrete points of incompatibility, as for example:

- The different interests, needs and desires
- The tools for the solution of the conflict
- The styles of contender and the way of negotiating

As we have seen, when in the middle of a troubled situation, we all respond in different ways. Moreover, we tend to react according to the context.

For example, the way we behave with our family is very often different to how we behave at the workplace. Nevertheless, in the majority of cases, we tend to have a principal style, a favorite style. Some people prefer competing and seeking to win at any expense. Others, on the contrary, always try to avoid the conflict, i.e., they get accommodated to the desires of "the Other".

Because of it, at the moment of intervening in an interpersonal conflict, it is crucial to understand not only those styles, but also the corresponding ways of negotiating and of solving a problem.

In many cases, people are not capable of approaching or settling their differences and consequently they resort to the help of a third person. The role of this middleman consists of helping the antagonists moving from a competitive style, accommodator or evader to a negotiating or collaborating approach.

This step, actually, will be possible only if people in conflict learn how to listen and to conceive the problem from other perspectives that are not theirs.

CHARACTERISTICS OF THE CONFLICTS

The conflicts can be split into several categories according to different characteristics, as each of them presents a distinctive feature.

Their recognition is of cardinal importance.

a) Depending on the number of participants:

A conflict may arise between two persons or may involve multiple parts as in the case of neighborhood problems.

When the parts involved in a conflict are more than two then exists the natural trend to form alliances between the parts, and this has to be born in mind for a positive conduction of the process. Those alliances can be more or less rigid, or can be constantly changing. This happens especially when the conflict is multiparty.

In this situation, very often, an alliance confronts the opposite party.

b) The solidity of the internal front:

If the members of one of the parts have between them some serious differences, those can turn out to be more difficult to face that the very problems they have with the "the Others".

The negotiation tends to become cumbersome due to the appearance of doubts, contradictions or controversies where nobody knows with certainty what is the point of view of "the Other".

c) Number of questions to be negotiated:

One of the most important elements to investigate when approaching a conflict is to determine what are the topics that we are going to tackle. Actually, the more topics into play the more difficult the reaching of a positive outcome will be.

This characteristic is very important because it is going to need some more of an active intervention from all the people that have interests in the conflict as well as from the very facilitator, whether there would be one.

d) The long lasting of the relations:

In our lives as well in groups or institutions, there is a very wide scale of relations depending on their permanency, their intensity, etc.

A classic example of lasting relations is the family relations. The spouses can divorce, but the children grant long lasting to the relation although in different terms. In the end, both spouses will be grandparents of the same grandsons.

But not only the family relations are lasting ones. Although with some minor intensity, the fact of dwelling in the same building, of being a company belonging to a certain guild, or being a professional from the same guild, are other examples. As we say, this characteristic has great transcendence to appropriately define the intervention in the conflict.

e) Imperious need (or not) for reaching an agreement:

Not all the conflicts possess the same level of need for reaching an agreement. Every case has its own pace. And these paces come determined by the content of what is discussed, in the internal paces or by the damage, personal or institutional, that a delay could yield.

In a company, discussing about where to locate the IT Department is not the same as discussing with a client over the delay in a foreseen date of payment.

An employee, putting another example, will discuss in a different way a salary rise with his boss depending whether he enjoys, or not, another income.

f) Those who negotiate need a guarantee:

This characteristic points at the independence of decision from those who face a negotiation. There are conflicts where the parts possess total autonomy on what they eventually decide, whereas in other conflicts the negotiator acts on behalf of someone or of a group. Those "clients" will be, in the end, those in charge of validating the offers put forward by the negotiators.

In general, people negotiate on their own account. When the person that negotiates assumes the highest hierarchy, it is predetermined that he concentrates the totality of the decision power.

When a couple gets divorced, when it is about personal obligations, when the family or friendship a relations are affected we can't wait for "the Other" to act. Although, actually, it is important to try not to damage the third party, one way or another, that could be affected by the adopted solution (it is the case of the children in a divorce or of our colleagues in a labour dispute).

g) The outcome will be compelling for both parts (or not):

When facing a conflict it is good to know if the agreement will be binding or not. Concretely, if the contending takes place at the Courts, the decision will bind the parts.

The same thing doesn't necessarily happen in particular agreements, which only express the will to carry out some action. In this situation, only if a breach exists will we need some legal homologation to start the process and make it effective.

Another different situation is given in the agreements between countries ruled by International Law, where the agreements are unstable due to the fulfillment of the decisions from third parties.

In a company we can distinguish (as an example):

- The disagreements between the Sales department and the Production department regarding some delivery date to a client, disagreements we can overcome through interchanges of ideas and information.
- The penalty that Human Resources applies to a member of the above-mentioned areas due to some breaches (for example, unjustified and repeated lack of punctuality, absences without previous notice, lack of collaboration, etc.)

h) Possibility of intervention from a third party:

According to the type of the conflict, the intervention of some impartial third persons can be feasible or not.

Concretely, when values come into play it is much more difficult to find a negotiator.

Therefore, the cause of the conflict determines the participation or not of a third party.

MODALITY

Here are detailed the aspects that form the frame where the conflict develops.

a) Public or private:

The fact that the negotiators are public or private, affects in a preponderant way a key aspect of any negotiation: the confidentiality of the initiated actions.

When the conflict comes to the public place, the presence of the public opinion can play a pivotal role, which forces the negotiators to work with special caution and evaluate the influence that the public opinion may have on any decision or proposal.

b) Primacy of formality over informality:
When the confrontation takes place within institutional areas ruled by laws and procedures, those aspects give the relation and moreover the conflict a more formal character.

Any resolution we achieve must bear these formal questions in mind in order that the approved conclusion is actually applicable.

On the contrary, if the conflicts between relatives, neighbors, colleagues, etc., occur in a more informal frame the search of the possible agreements implies a major range of possibilities.

In both cases, feelings are put into play, but the possibilities of working with them are different in each case.

c) Degree of violence prior to the negotiation:
When we intervene in a conflict, using any of the possible methods of resolution at hand, it is most important to know the degree of violence reached prior sitting down and negotiating.

We refer here both to physical violence and to psychological violence. Although both are negative and have to be taken in consideration, the former tends to hinder the relation much more and makes the posterior intervention much more difficult.

If we think of international conflicts, we will appreciate this modality with major clarity. It is not the same when two countries fight in the international courts performing verbal aggressions, as when they directly unleash a war.

The same correlation between violence and major complexity of the conflict is also, actually, present in all interpersonal relations.

Part 2
The positive management of conflicts

WHY ARE CONFLICTS UNWISHED?

Solving a conflict supposes to reduce, eliminate or terminate it. Managing a conflict, on the other hand, has to deal more with designing a series of strategies that try to minimize the negative aspects of the conflict and, eventually, with promoting its positive aspects. Within a company we would speak of improving the efficiency of the team, of the Department or even of the whole organization.

We have already exposed that, here, different approximations converge. There are some persons who think that conflicts must be eradicated at all costs although other managers think that their teams bask too much into homogeneous thinking and so they struggle to promote some degree of conflict between them.

Our attitude concerning this dilemma revolves around bearing in mind the type of conflict we are talking about. There are conflicts that we must eradicate as soon as they appear, whereas another type of conflicts is not only convenient but also desirable.

Among the aspects that make the conflict an unwished situation in an organization we can mention the following ones:

- The competitive processes. The perception of incompatible motives drives to the need to prevail on " "the Other"" to reach our own aims. The aims don't have necessarily to be incompatible, but when they are

so perceived it is more than probable that they lead to an escalation of the conflict.
- <u>Biases and distortions</u>. When a conflict intensifies, the perceptions tend to distort. The information is understood in a binary way from one perspective or from another. What is identified as belonging to the opponent is discarded.
- <u>Emotions</u>. The conflicts tend to expose such emotions as anxiety, irritation, anger or frustration. The emotions tend to dominate the rational thinking and turn us into "irrational" persons.
- <u>Impoverishment of the communication</u>. We communicate less with the people that displease us, and more with people that please us. Communication turns into a tool for defeating, denigrating or discrediting the point of view of the interlocutor, in order to strengthen our own.
- <u>Confused topics</u>. The central topic becomes confused and not well defined. Often, we reach a point where the parts don't know why the conflict began in the first place and what they were claiming at first.
- <u>Rigid commitments</u>. The parts entrench in their positions.
- <u>The differences are maximized and the similarities are minimized</u>. One tends to see "the Other" as radically opposite.
- <u>Escalation of the conflict</u>. When the parts narrow down their points of view, they become more intolerant, put more into defensive mode and become more emotional. Every part tries more to conquer "the Other" than to achieve his own aims. The conflict escalates.

It is not surprising, therefore, that when in an organization we find many conflicts those have a series of negative consequences:

- Tension and stress, at least in the involved persons. Also frustration and hostility as a consequence of the blocking of the aspirations.
- They can produce inadequate redistributions of the resources.
- If the conflict sharpens, the energies can move towards aims that are not actual organizational managing issues hence leading to a malfunctioning of the company.
- The conflict can also affect the fulfillment of the aims.
- It may provoke delays in the communication, impoverishment of the collaboration style and cohesion and, as a consequence of it, stalling of the core activity.

For all this, to approach the conflict it is necessary to begin by knowing the circumstances where it takes place, how they affect each of the parts and what behaviors they put into play during the conflict. In other words, to tackle a conflict the first thing that it is necessary to do is understand it. It is extremely difficult to confront the solution of a conflictive situation if we don't know what it is about and how it has developed. The knowledge of all those elements will help us determine which conflicts must be eliminated and which could even be stimulated.

We will stress, once again, the transcendence that the perception aspects play at the moment of living the conflict one way or another. The way the involved persons explain the conflict where they are immersed provides some very valuable information about how they live through it and what they think about it.

In practice, there are diverse methods to manage the conflict.

As we have already said, one of the methods most used in many organizations is based on the belief that if it is left alone, the conflict will take care of itself. In our opinion, this one is the less advisable position to adopt. Ignoring the conflict can lead to:

- Increase the indignation and the resentment of the parts.
- Perpetuate the "we have always done it that way".
- Suffocate new ideas.

Consequently, our conviction is that in all cases it is necessary to manage the conflict. As we were saying a few paragraphs above, when we say "managing" we mean the utilization of strategies and tactics to lead the parts towards the resolution or, at least, towards the containment of the dispute so we avoid the escalation of the conflict and the destruction of the relations.

We have mentioned it previously, but we consider relevant to reaffirm it. The dysfunctional conflict:

- Costs money
- Entrails risks
- Degrades the quality of the decisions

It is for this reason that, at this point, someone needs to step forward and help solving the conflict.

Another way of managing a conflict is when one of the involved parts tries to tackle it individually. For example, the person can decide to attack the so-viewed opponent, or accept some offers from the interlocutor or even adopt some positions before the adversary just in case.

For us, nevertheless, the principal path to satisfactorily solve any conflict is the pacific path. The violent, aggressive, harmful ways, the will to win at any price and to make the interlocutor eventually lose will complicate the conflict and habitually escalate it.

The violent reaction denies the conflict: it pretends to eliminate "the Other", it ignores his humanity and his personal dignity and imposes a false solution through the use of force (punishment, insult, physical mistreatment, humiliation ...). This situation, in the majority of the cases, provokes lack of communication, deep wounds, mutual distrust, resentment, fears, need of revenge, clash and feeling of injustice.

Actually, a pacific living together doesn't mean not having conflicts at all, but it is what remains after solving them pacifically. The group or persons' community where the conflicts don't exist makes us suspect of if actually those latter are actually ignored or concealed.

To be able to deal with the conflicts, there is a series of previous necessary conditions. If those don't apply, the conflicts can remain sealed and secret. In order that this doesn't happen, we have to:

- Assume that the conflict is an opportunity to learning instead of a threat to a harmonious living. This is part of the process of justice: " *They are placing me in a situation I have not looked for, OK, so I am going to try to get the most benefit and extract some profitable learning*". This might seem quite philosophical but undoubtedly it is highly constructive.
- Admit that there exists a conflict, that there is something that doesn't work.
- Recognize yourself as a part of it. Often we think that the problem is caused by the interlocutor, not by us. We tend to self-excuse and to cast the fault on the interlocutor.

- Have the will for dialogue: you want to see what happens, to be ready to mutually listen and to strain for looking for agreements. Willing to talk is recognizing "the Other", accepting his dignity and his right to think and to feel (although in a different way from ours). Not having the intention of talking supposes the opposite.
- Have the will for solution seeking from both parts. For this it is necessary to know the mutual needs and to look for solutions of mutual benefit, according to which both parts turn out to be winners. In this process, it is critical to keep the emotional part of our brain under control.

To transform a conflict, we have to put into play a series of skills as well as generate and modify some attitudes. The following picture reflects some of the attitudes we find in the conflicts. As the reader will verify, the attitudes that appear don't precisely favor the management of the conflict, although, unfortunately, they are pretty frequent.

ACTIONS NOT TO BE TAKEN

To give orders: To tell the interlocutor what he must do

- "You have to..."
- "You must do..."

To threaten: To tell the interlocutor what may happen to him if he doesn't do what is asked from him

- "Do this, otherwise..."
- "You better do what I ask you, if not..."

To sermonize: To allude to an external norm to say what "the Other" must do

- "You must be responsible…"
- "Men don't cry…"

To patronize: To allude to our experience to say what is good or bad for the interlocutor

- "The nowadays so-called professionals have very small commitment, in my time they used to fully commit themselves"

To advise: To tell the interlocutor what is the best thing for him

- The best thing you can do is…
- Leave this team; it is the best thing for you…

To console: To minimize what the interlocutor feels or wants

- "Let it be …"
- "Don't worry.…"

To approve: To give reason to the interlocutor

- I agree with you, the best thing is that…

To disapprove: To rebuke the interlocutor

- "What you are saying is a bilge…"
- "What you are doing doesn't make sense."

To insult: To despise the interlocutor for what he says or does

- "That happens to you for being gullible."
- "What a stupidity what you are saying."
- "You are not capable of anything better"

To interpret: To tell the interlocutor the secret motive of his attitude

- "In the end you want to draw attention."
- "Actually you want some other thing."

To interrogate: To extract information from the interlocutor
- When, where, why?
- "What did he say about this person?"

To ironize: To jeer the interlocutor
- "Yeah, right, quit your job and start panhandling on the streets"
- "Do men act that way?"

It is perfectly possible to acquire any of the skills that are necessary to manage a conflict, as well as to develop them. Although in a posterior section we will expose in depth those skills, here comes a first outline:

- <u>Humanize the conflict</u>: accept that the interlocutor can think and feel in a different way than us; i.e., in essence recognize "the Other" as a person.
- <u>Develop empathy</u>: put yourself in the place of the interlocutor, try to understand what he thinks and feels. Only that way is it possible to respect his position (though it doesn't mean necessarily that we share it).

- <u>Listen openly, attentively</u>. If we think that we are knowledgeable of what happens to the interlocutor, we can be wrong provided that often we will lack important information. Very often, we believe that we know many things about "the Other" before having even listened to him.
- <u>Be assertive</u>: express with respect and with clarity what you think and what you feel without attacking, offending or ashaming the interlocutor.
- <u>Have some disposition to giving away</u> some of our claims in order to come to satisfactory agreements for both parts: both parts win although we "lose" something.
- <u>Possess some degree of self-criticism</u>: recognize that, in spite of having our own reasons, we can be wrong. Our interlocutor, in the end, may also have his own reasons.
- <u>Use creativity</u>: imagine different solutions, so you may be in a better disposition to pick the best.

The parts involved in a conflict may decide to manage their conflicts together, i.e., without resorting to anybody else. This process is named negotiation. About what it is about is reconciling apparently incompatible interests.

The mediation or conciliation is the meeting of the parts in a propitious environment and under some concrete circumstances to try to reach an agreement. The conciliator is essentially a facilitator of the communication process between the parts in conflict.

The role of the mediator is, on the other hand, more active, as he can put forward offers, intervene openly in the discussions and even propose suggestions with the intention of coming to an agreement.

In the arbitration, one of the most traditional conflicts solving method, someone plays the role of an umpire and has the power to take decisions on the agreement, which are eventually binding for the parts.

We will come back to all this. But before, we are going to expose a couple of very simple models, which, in spite of their simplicity, can provide us with some tremendously valuable guidelines for understanding and tackling the conflicts.

"OLD" BRAIN VS "NEW" BRAIN

From our point of view, this theoretical model can help us face the conflict with more possibilities of success.

The North American neuroscientist MacLean presented his evolutionary theory of the triple brain, which proposes that the human brain, in its origin, was formed actually by three brains in one: the reptilian, the limbic and the neocortex.

The reptilian or basic brain is characterized by being the cradle of the basic "intelligence", the intelligence of the routines and of the rituals. Its processes are unconscious and automatic.

That brain controls the breathing, the cardiac pulse, and the blood pressure and even collaborates in the continuous expansion – contraction of our muscles.

The reptilian brain acts especially as a life guardian, as in it resides the sense of survival and of struggle. This first brain is our adviser of dangers for the body in general and allows adjustment with rapidity by means of elementary and uncomplicated answers, both emotionally and intellectually.

In synthesis, this most primitive part of our brain takes charge of the basic instincts of survival (sexual desire, the search for food and the aggressive answers of the type "fight or fly").

The limbic brain, on the other hand, is the home of the emotions, of the affective and motivacional intelligence. Here are the roots of the centers of affectability and it is where the different emotions are experienced and where the human beings we experience sorrow, distresses and intense happy moments.

Throughout evolution, to the instincts, impulses and emotions brain was added the neocortex, also called rational brain, which incorporates the aptitude to think in an abstract form and beyond the immediacy of the present moment, to understand the existing global relations, and to develop conscious and complex emotional life.

The cerebral crust, the newest and most important zone of the human brain, covers and wraps the oldest and primitive core. It is important to bear in mind, nevertheless, that those latter regions have not been eliminated; they just remain deep down below, not owning the undisputed control of the body, although remaining perfectly active.

In fact, in conflicts, this is precisely the principal problem. In front of a troubled situation (i.e. generating emotions and therefore triggering instinctive acts), the old brain is the one that happens to take control, to "give orders".

When an event is processed through this emotional system, it is very difficult to think coolly and logically. It is extremely difficult to avoid rapid and brainless conclusions on the task in question or on those persons that have opinions opposite to ours.

Temperamental system	Calm system
Emotional	Cognitive
"To go"	"To know"
Simple	Complex
Spontaneous	Reflexive
Quick	Slow
Develops early	Develops later
Accentuated by the stress	Attenuated by the stress

The temperamental system is emotional and impulsive. It sets itself free through stimuli that lead to instantaneous reactions instead of to reflection and reasoning. The calm system, on the other hand, is the basis of the self-management and self-control.

In stressful situations, and conflict is one of them, our temperamental system is activated by everything, which implies that essentially we unleash emotional reactions that will impede a well-argued conversation. As soon as the emotions have freed themselves, they very rarely get spontaneously back in the box.

What is the key then? Learning a series of practices that should help us face the conflicts in a productive form and develop the requested collateral skills. One of the most important practices has to deal with the skill for examinating and transforming thoughts and feelings that hamper our aptitude to coolly reason when the conflicts arise.

No doubt, we all can learn to manage the thoughts and the feelings that surface when the conflict is managed.

That implies thinking about our reactions and re-defining the situation, thus being less prone to unwanted emotions and, hereby, being in better disposition to raise questions and to consider the alternative interpretations. In other words, we have to be first capable of managing ourselves before trying to manage a conflict.

SIMPLIFIED TRANSACTIONAL ANALYSIS

Don't be afraid, dear reader! We don't want to enter in depth this methodology of humanist psychology named transactional analysis. Nevertheless, we are sure that a couple of ideas extracted from that model can help us manage the conflicts more adequately.

At a functional level, the transactional analysis seeks to facilitate the analysis of the ways in which people interact. For it we use three states: Father, Adult and Child. The first one is used for caring, the second one for steadying ourselves and the third one for seeking and receiving care, both in our interaction with "the Other", as with ourselves.

Nevertheless, there are several "interactions" that tend to block the resolution of the conflict. We refer to all the combinations between Father and Child. In other words, the only combinations that help us move forward in the resolution of the conflict are those that include an assertive Adult.

Father: a state where people behave, feel and think in a response to an unconscious imitation of how their parents (or other parental figures) acted or how they interpreted the actions of their parents. For example, someone can yell at someone out of frustration, because in his infancy "he "learned" from an influential figure the lesson that this very behavior could be deemed as a form of effective relation.

Adult: a state that is like an artifact for processing information and realizing predictions, where the principal emotions that might affect its proper functioning are absent (or at least controlled). While we are in the state of Adult, we can perform an objective evaluation of the reality.

Child: a state where people behave in a way similar to how they did during their infancy. For example, someone who receives an unfavorable evaluation at work can respond by pouting and staring at his shoes, even start weeping, as probably he used to do when he was scolded when a child. On the contrary, someone who receives a good review can respond with a wide smile and a gesture of gratefulness. The Child, in other words, is the source of the emotions, of creation, of recreation, of spontaneity and of intimacy.

In those situations where we think that we are behaving as Adult but still have prejudices, it is actually the Internal Father who is acting without having an Adult conscience of it. My Adult will be contaminated if he takes as a fact what my Father was thinking without actually investigating it.

Adult can be contaminated by Child. For example, if I have the illusory belief that people are against me when actually they are not, it could be that my internal Child is contaminating my thinking as Adult.

Another very common internal problem is exclusion. It takes place when we allow one of the states to act or express in a rigid form for too long. In this situation, we are constantly acting as "Father" or constantly as "Adult" or constantly as "Child" at the cost of not acting as a full human being.

What we suggest, after this model outlining, and along with the line of the previous model of "the three brains", is that the reader makes sure that before a conflict, Adult acts in an assertive form in front of a Father or a Child. With this attitude we will manage "to "hoist" both old parts from the old brain up to the new brain and, that way, be able to start negotiating rationally a satisfactory solution to the conflict.

ASSERTIVENESS: A KEY SKILL

Assertiveness is a form of conscious, coherent, clear, direct and balanced expression, which purpose is to communicate our ideas and feelings or to defend our legitimate rights without the intention of hurting or of harming, acting out of an interior state of self-confidence, instead of resorting to the typical hampering limitations due for instance to anxiety or to anger.

It is therefore a style of communication open to foreign opinions, granting the same importance to theirs and to ours. It is about showing some respect towards both "the Other" and ourselves, putting forward safely and confidently what we want, accepting that the attitude of "the Other" doesn't have to coincide with ours and avoiding unnecessary conflicts in a direct, open and honest form.

Assertiveness allows us to say what we actually think, thus acting in consequence, doing what we consider to be best adapted to us, defending our rights, interests or needs without attacking or offending anybody, and not permitting to be attacked or offended, and eventually avoiding situations that cause us anxiety.

Assertiveness can be seen as a negotiation, a consensus or an agreement with the interlocutor so that both parts get benefited.

As the reader will have already hinted, assertiveness is one of the key skills for conflicts management. It is this personal skill that allows us express our feelings, opinions and thoughts, in the opportune moment, in a direct form, honestly and without disrespect towards the rights of "the Other".

- Direct. It presupposes that our affirmations don't imply any "double entendre". The manifestation that we realize is clear and doesn't have any pretension to manipulate. We don't beat around the bush.
- Honest. It implies that our behavior is coherent. Our words, our tone of voice and our corporal language consistently express the very same thing. We show a direct visual contact and at the same time, a relaxed body attitude.
- Adapted: Our expression takes in account the rights and the feelings of our interlocutor. And, obviously also our feelings. The moment and the place of expressing those affirmations are adequate.

In spite of the transcendence of our aptitude to express an assertive message, it is also fundamental that our aptitude to assimilate what "the Others" express or communicate and, especially, our skill not to react in a way that denies them the right to express their ideas or feelings.

We all should be capable of listening attentively to the commentaries of "the Other", may that be expressions of dissatisfaction or commentaries where they expose their expectations. Though, actually it is not simple, it is perfectly possible to listen to the discomfort or the dissatisfaction that "the Other" expresses towards us without reacting with bad manners or with defensive expressions.

In fact, one of the keys when strong emotions appear in the conversation consists of supporting precisely the open dialogue to try to verify what is what the interlocutor exactly tries to say.

In those cases, we all have seen (and probably experienced) that a bad-tempered reply or an incisive denial uses to send the tension over the roof and, with all probability, minimizes the possibilities of supporting a posterior dialogue.

Whatever we are assertive or not, we all have a series of rights that we must have very present in mind at the moment of applying any skill.

- Free to express our opinions and our ideas (provided that doing so we don't violate the rights of "the Other")
- The right to see our ideas and opinions respected
- The right to be wrong (provided that we accept the posterior responsibility derived from our acts)
- The right to change our mind (to say "I don't know", or to look for information to verify what has happened in a specific situation)
- The right to ask
- The right to choose the moment when to act

Being fully conscious of all of those rights liberates us from the emotional explosions of "the Other" and, actually, allows us express and adapt our opinions and our ideas. That way, we can be of more help to "the Other".

Why do we stress here these aspects? Essentially, because often we verify how many people (some of them managers with numerous reports) before any conflict choose to act passively and let the conflict self solve.

One of the reasons for this proceeding owes to that many people have the belief that they have to be nice, polite or considerate with "the Other". And, obviously, they take this belief way too far. Up to such a point that often, they decide to silent their ideas, not to expose their points of view or accept behaviors from "the Other" that are, by all means, unjustified and can even suppose that the conflict is even more exacerbated.

The second reason why we decide not to act in situations of conflict responds to the firm and established belief that if we act then "the Other" will not understand it. Under the influence of this belief, we choose not to speak openly, to conceal our feelings and opinions that the behavior provokes on "the Other". In the end, there sublies a zealous attitude to protecting "the Other" which helps us justify our passiveness before the conflict.

Evidently, when acting that way, what we actually express is the fact that we harbor very low expectations about the capacity of the interlocutor to adopt a mature behavior before the conflict. Because of it, we assume the responsibility for the feelings of "the Other".

Nevertheless, it is good to always bear in mind the following affirmation: we are not by any means responsible for the feelings of "the Other" and, therefore, we cannot accept any responsibility for the way other persons relate to us. "The Others" are people accountable for their own behaviors.

Then, why do so many people insist on acting in a way practically opposite to what rationally should be done? Basically this proceeding owes to those reasons:

- To get things done

Often the conflict spontaneously abates, truth to be said. Nevertheless, thinking of the long term, that tactic tends to lead to the appearance of a buried and subtle hostility between the parts.

- To feel good

In other occasions, we think that with a simple anger outburst the conflict will end, and besides we even think that this alleviation will make us feel good. Actually, we cannot speak about correct or incorrect feelings; however we think that what we decide to do with our feelings is make them effective or ineffective. As we will see, in practically all situations, describing what happens inside us turns out to be much more effective that expressing those feelings without any control.

- Because everything has a limit

It uses to happen in persons that behaved passively during some time (maybe with standing grievances and dissatisfactions) and that, come to a point, feel justified to lose their temper (even because of a non transcendental situation).

Unfortunately, the ire of those persons do not always keeps relation with the dimension of the incident and, obviously, is not always aimed towards the proper person (in fact, very rarely). In any case, when an emotional reaction of this nature takes place, we tend to lose respect.

Another way of seeing things consists of thinking about what we can do and what we can contribute to. We all have our own resources: knowledge, feelings, and behaviors. A manager, for example, has some information and points of view to share, some needs and feelings to expose, critiques and recognitions to express and, actually, decisions to adopt. If we put into play our resources in a direct, honest and adequate form we will be in a better disposition to tackle the conflicts in a more effective way.

Our aim should be to achieve an open communication, without the emotions dominating the interchanges, without anxieties or manipulations from any of the parts. With this approach, it is much more feasible that, before any conflict, we propitiate the cooperation, we induce to action and to the eradication of the conflict. The most transcendent thing, all in all, is to be conscious that all of this is never achieved through abandonment of our rights (not facing the conflict) and actually not trampling on the rights of "the Other" either.

Besides being assertive, what other things can we do to tackle a conflict?

HOW TO TRANSMIT THAT WE ARE LIVING A CONFLICT?

GIVE INFORMATION

As we were previously saying, when providing information we should strain for complying with a series of requirements: being direct, descriptive, impartial and avoiding giving advice.

- Be direct. Give information as just plain information. I.e., provide concrete and neutral information, without standing out or despising what we want our opponent to do (or stop doing). With this approach, we are treating "the Other" as a responsible individual and capable of extracting his own conclusions.
- Be descriptive. The more details about the situation we put forward, the better. If the information we put forward is of a too general character, it is possible that the interlocutor doesn't know how to interpret this information, and, which is worse, doesn't ask us for any additional explanation to clear his doubts.
- Be impartial. It is important not to value the information that we are putting forward and,

moreover, to make sure of not expressing any threat (although it might be implicit). Otherwise we would block the posterior analysis of the topic.
- Don't give advice. This is probably one of the most difficult actions to take. Specially, in the context of people management. Many managers think, most likely wrongly, that telling "the Other" how they have to behave is the right way of acting. Much on the contrary, this kind of behavior generates dependence and, what's worse, very poor acceptance of the solution we propose to ending up the conflict.

TO GIVE OUR OPINION OR OUR POINT OF VIEW

Another action that we might take to tackle the conflict is giving our opinion or our point of view. When giving our opinion or point of view we suggest:
- To stand for our rights. As we have previously mentioned, we are wholly entitled to have a personal opinion and point of view. Independently of whether we might be right or wrong.
- To know what we want to say (make ourselves hear). We have to make sure that our ideas and our points of view on the conflict are sufficiently clear. If we don't have a formed opinion yet, we should try to previously clarify the topics or even expose our point of view in a tentative way ("*it is difficult for me to understand that ...*"). As well, we can agree or disagree with what other persons involved in the conflict have said and, actually, modify the direction of the conversation ("*I believe that you are forgetting an important information and it is that ...*").

- To realize affirmations that begin with "I". Given its importance, we will return on this point later. Basically we talk of personalizing our ideas or points of view.
- Not to apologize. We have the whole right to have our own point of view and we don't have to apologize because of it.
- Not to intimidate. We have already seen that the right way of exposing our point of view is, simply, doing it in a direct and descriptive way. Asking in an inquisitive way or taking sides debilitates considerably our point of view and, especially, provokes that our interlocutor puts even more on the defensive. Precisely because of that, it is much more effective to expose with clarity our point of view. Besides, doing it so favors that the process of communication can be kept open.

TO EXPOSE OUR NEEDS AND OUR DESIRES

When doing so it is important:

- To know perfectly what we want. It is fundamental to centre with clarity on what we want to obtain from the situation. For example: what concrete behaviors will "the Other" have to show, what commitments we want people involved in the conflict to adopt, when do they have to adopt those behaviors or those commitments, etc.
- To put forward our suppositions. "The Other" cannot read our thoughts. Because of that, exposing our suppositions is transcendental. Often, besides, when presenting our truth we do it in a very generic way and so "the Other" doesn't necessarily interpret it the way we think he should do. Hence the most effective strategy is

about exposing our suppositions in a clear, simple and direct way.
- Encourage people to answer. In all this process, as we said, it is important to be clear and succinct. Therefore, after exposing the information and our needs and desires, we should make a pause and hope that the interlocutor says something. If the interlocutor doesn't jump in, we should strain to provoke his intervention. Why? Just to know if he has listened to us, if he has understood us and to which extent is our demand accepted or not. Assuming —without double-checking— that those three actions have taken place (or even just one) constitutes one of the worst mistakes in the communication process.
- On the other hand, when facing difficult and inconvenient situations (and the conflict does fit this description) many of us tend to accelerate our communication process, to finish it as soon as possible because of the unpleasantness of the situation. Because of that, the majority of us tend to express just a few things or do it in a too vehement form.
- Obviously, if we allow ourselves to walk that path, our intervention tends to turn into a monologue. That leads to the non-acceptance and the non-commitment of the interlocutor towards a solution.
- Let's not shoot ourselves in the foot. In some occasions, it seems that we are expressing this type of behavior: We say "no" to ourselves even before starting speaking with the person with whom we are in conflict. When we initiate a phrase saying: "*I know that I should not ask you that ...*" we are predisposing the interlocutor to not even consider our opinion.
- As we were saying, if we have decided to tackle a conflict, we should have previously pondered what we want the

interlocutor to do in this situation and, especially, why it is important that he does it.

TO EXPOSE OUR FEELINGS

When exposing our feelings it is good to bear in mind the following:

- Recognize what our feelings are. For most persons this doesn't turn out to be simple. In fact, we tend to live way too much separated from them. Nevertheless, exposing to the interlocutor what our feelings are in relation to the conflict will facilitate us establish a more genuine contact with "the Other". For that, we have to realize a declaration in the first person of the type: " *I feel that ...*", "*I have the sensation that ...*". We are not saying that doing this is simple. And it is also not easy to untie if from what constitutes the expression of an opinion or a point of view. We use to be very good in beginning the phrases saying, "*I believe that ...*", but beginning that way we are not exposing anything of what we feel. The good news, nevertheless, is that this type of expressions, with some practice, can integrate our habitual repertoire provided that we assume a full conscience of their usefulness.

TO EXPLAIN OUR FEELINGS

- Relaxingly explaining what happens to us without being driven by our emotions demonstrates respect for "the Other"; and, at the same time, showing strong self-control. Then "the Other" sees that for a start we don't despise his feelings, ensuing thus that the possibilities of continuing the conversation are much higher. On the other hand, having feelings and expressing them openly is actually absolutely legitimate. As we have repeatedly mentioned, respect is the basic condition for the maintenance of a dialogue. Without respect, it is not possible to move forward and, besides, when the latter is absent, the positions turn out to be extreme. Actually, whenever talking to someone it is fundamental to keep open the process of communication. It is of great help to keep in mind that other persons also possess information, have opinions and defend legit points of view. If we talk about conflict, being conscious of this circumstance is even more critic. Hence listening and considering the opinion of "the Other" turns out to be basic when tackling a conflict. Contrarily to what many people think, this proceeding has not to deal with agreeing or not with "the Other". And even less, with making ourselves responsible for the issues of "the Other". With this kind of approach it is much more probable than we understand the vision of the interlocutor about the conflict, and from there on, eventually, we will have the possibility of modifying the current behavior and of looking for the future commitment of that person.

HOW TO FIND OUT ABOUT THE VISION OF "THE OTHER" ABOUT THE UNDERGOING CONFLICT?

Let's see now some of the skills that it is good to put into play when finding out about the interlocutor's vision about the conflict:

LOOKING FOR INFORMATION

It is fundamental to start by knowing what has happened. Or at least, try to compile all the information that we can gather on the matter. For that reason it would be suitable to follow a series of steps that you will find logical enough:

- Prepare ourselves adequately. Before having the meeting with the person, it is important to gather the major quantity of information about the situation and the person. With this we are trying to analyze the background, the precedents of the conflict and the behaviors expressed by the opposite party.
- Formulate questions. We need information but we also need that "the Other" exposes his feelings and his opinions. Definitively, we require that the interlocutor provide us with his vision of the conflict and especially how he is living through it. As it is easy to suppose, the information that we obtain will depend indeed on the environment that we have

been capable of creating and at the same time on the type and quality of the questions we formulate. For example, it is of supreme usefulness to formulate the questions (one question at a time) and to make ourselves sure that the tone of those questions doesn't contain any underlying evaluative background. This impression is difficult to avoid if we start with a *"why ...?"*. Whenever we initiate with this interrogative pronoun "the Other" uses to awkwardly shift in his seat, putting on the defensive and, finally, tends to answer to his behavior with justifications. Let's not dismiss the fact that, at any moment, we have to realize an evaluation, which is a fundamental step to move towards the treatment of the conflict. What we want to say is that, in any case, it is not important to realize an evaluation of the situation until having put under the spotlight the feelings, the impressions and the opinions about the conflict of the person with whom we are speaking.

TO LISTEN

It is something easy to say but tremendously difficult to do, at least fully.

- Listen without judging. The appropriate thing is to realize our evaluation once we have listened, not before. Truth is that we tend to hurry up to extract conclusions in spite of the fact that, in no few circumstances, this behavior is highly ineffective. In many conflicts, besides, it is habitual that one of the people involved is not really conscious of his behavior or of his attitude.

In consequence, he doesn't have any knowledge of the impact of his actions or attitudes on "the Other" either.
- Paraphrase. This is, to repeat in our own words the essence of the speech we listened to. Before acting in any conflict, we need to be very sure of the situation and of all the aspects of the conflict. Expressing what we believe having understood empowers our credibility and forms the perception in the mind of the interlocutor that we are really interested in him as a human being.

Some possible phrases to initiate could be:

- You want to say that ...?
- I understand that...
- In other words....
- You think then...
- Then what you are telling me is that...

Verify the validity of your interpretation; some possible phrases can be similar to:

- Is this correct?
- Is it this what you want to say to me?
- Did I understand you properly?
- Does this sum up what you have told me?

When paraphrasing, it is important to include those questions, because, by doing so, the interlocutor has the possibility of modifying his explanation, of extending or correcting it. With this, besides giving us a more precise idea about what our opponent has really tried to say, we demonstrate our good predisposition to support an open and two-ways communication avoiding us to emotionally react to the contents that he is exposing to us.

SHOW EMPATHY

Empathy has to deal with showing our interlocutor that we understand his feelings, that we understand him as a person. To demonstrate empathy we suggest:

- To recognize the feelings. Though it doesn't always happen, it is relatively habitual that when we express our vision of a conflict we do it with raw emotions. Because of this, the fact of recognizing the feelings of that person has great transcendence. This action bears two well-differentiated facets: first listen and then understand. It is good to underline again that understanding the feelings of someone has nothing to do with agreeing with those feelings. It is perfectly feasible to acknowledge the feelings of our interlocutor without judging them (for example, the frustration of someone because of the repellent body odor of a colleague) and, at the same time, express our disagreement with the action, when the collaborator vents out its frustration by insulting that person.
- To reflect the feelings. Reflecting is pretty much related to paraphrasing. In this case, it is about expressing aloud our interpretation of the emotional tone that we have perceived in the interlocutor and that defines his feelings (*"you are fed up"*, *"you feel frustrated"*, *"you are overwhelmed"*). Initially, this proceeding helps the communication process to move on, and the interlocutor will perceive that we worry about him as a person. Besides, with this proceeding, normally that person will confirm us whether our understanding of his emotional tone is correct (what would constitute a magnificent confirmation of our perception) or, in its defect, will nuance or add some additional

element that will complete our vision of his mindset. This happens to many people. Habitually, we are not that much accustomed to work with feelings. In fact, those have been systematically ostracized by the organizations as considering them not relevant with the aspects of task or with the attainment of aims. Nothing wronger than that. Feelings exercise a crucial influence and, in fact, determine our actions. Especially, in situations of conflict. Consequently, if we don't pay the due attention to the feelings involved in a conflict we will lose the opportunity to obtain an essential information that we undoubtedly will need to properly tackle the conflict.

Accept the critiques

To demonstrate that we accept the critiques we suggest:

- Not to react to them. Provided that the critiques are pertinent to our performance, they do help us. Let's contemplate every critique as a real gift. Actually, we are not saying that accepting critiques is easy. The most habitual behavior before them is to react with justifications or, come to the case, with a counter-attack. It is undoubtedly a standard human reaction, although it is true that this said behavior is poorly effective. And we know it. Before this proceeding, the communication flow ends up abruptly and, as a consequence of it, we cannot know the feelings, the data and the information that reside in the heart of the conflict. What do we propose then? Simply to pay attention and to carefully analyze the critiques we receive. We can even formulate questions with the intention of exploring more in depth the critique that has just been put forward. Something like *"why do you say it?"*. In any case, the key thing is that whenever we intervene the interlocutor perceives neither a threat nor a self-justification.

- To request suggestions. It is perfectly logical that once analyzed the critique, we look for alternatives and, in that case, request suggestions. "The Other" can help us at that moment. Asking for help is not, far from it, a weakness. Very much on the contrary, it generates closeness and, besides, it is very probable that, when done, "the Other" provides us with some estimable ideas.

- To recognize our mistakes. If we have committed some mistake, it is important to recognize it. In a clear and unambiguous way. We all are fallible and we can commit mistakes, although that doesn't exempt us from accepting the responsibility of the consequences, always in a positive and productive form. We also have to anticipate the fact that probably not all of the critiques are going to be expressed in a rational form. Often these will be notably hostile, sarcastic or just inappropriate. In those cases, it will not be possible to analyze them in depth, so we will not accept that critique (for example, we can decide to say something like *"Maybe it is just like that"*) or even decide to remain quiet. The prevailing idea, in any case, is not to play the game our interlocutor is playing. Otherwise we would be reacting and losing our self-control capacity. We would not gain anything with that whereas on the other hand, we might lose a lot (time, energy, confidence, etc.).

THE NON-VERBAL COMMUNICATION IN THE CONFLICTS

A communication is considered to be complete when the emitted message matches the received message.

In spite of what we might think, we are always communicating something. As "it is impossible not to communicate" there is never an emptiness of meaning. In some occasions, we ignore the subtle messages or are not fully conscious of them, but we are always transmitting something.

We transmit messages with the tone of voice that nuances our words, with our specific facial gestures, with what we stop doing or insist on continuing doing while the interlocutor speaks and, also, often, even when not saying anything.

People who spend some time coexisting together manage to develop some communication "keys". Some words or phrases turn often into symbols of messages of major proportions.

Nevertheless, when we don't know "the Other" very well, it is more difficult to decode his messages.

In fact, the relations between people often deteriorate due to the fact that the involved parts react to the unconscious messages that are transmitted, without knowing with clarity what provoked their response. The interlocutor, also unaware of the subtle level of the messages he has transmitted, will perceive the behavior of "the Other" as irrational or as a sign of aggressiveness or lack of disposition to make things improve. If we stop to think, even the very context where the interaction develops also contains some meaning for people (because of it, to manage the conflict is very important to select very cautiously the place where the conversation is going to take place).

Therefore, provided that it is impossible "not to communicate", we should always wonder: what is exactly what I am understanding about everything that happens between us? Sharing the above-mentioned interpretation with the interlocutor guarantees the opportunity to clarify any misunderstanding, besides helping the interlocutor identify the subtlest aspects of his communication.

Key sentence

When there are inconsistencies between the verbal and the non-verbal message, the non-verbal message almost always has more impact that the uttered word.

The words that we pick can often be manipulated, diluted, disguised and leading to misrepresentation. Think for a moment about the debates between politicians.

Roughly, the non-verbal signs occupy approximately 60 % of the content of the message in any interpersonal communication. In consequence, if we stop paying attention to the above-mentioned signs, our communication can be vague and terribly confusing.

Obviously, the most complex situations about communication and, hence, the most propitious to trigger potential conflicts, take place in environments where people spend a lot of time together (for example, at the workplace, in a couple, in a family circle, etc.).

In fact, remember that we can "cheat" some people during some time, though it is much more improbable to achieve it with our partner (for example) all the time, simply because the latter has innumerable opportunities "to catch us" in an incoherence in our communication.

Continuing with the example, when a couple strains for achieving a more satisfactory relation, usually the husband says to his wife: " *I am listening. I understand*", while he looks in another direction or stares at the floor. Probably the tone of his voice, but especially his non-verbal communication (in this case, the look) is indicating apathy and thus he is actually transmitting a message like this: " *same old story. Same old neurotic*!"

This is so because in spite of what he is saying (the message, the very words), his wife reacts stronger to the non-verbal signs than to the very verbal communication. In fact, she gets angry before the apparent physical nonchalance of her husband.

From here on we all know what finally happens (in the context of a couple or in any other context). As the agitation of the wife increases, the husband starts mumbling and generally abandons the battlefield (well, provided that he has an escape route). We get a negative feedback and the environment becomes toxic. We are in a dead-end alley (or in one with a very difficult exit).

Because of this, it is extremely important to assume the responsibility of every message we express, be it verbal or non-verbal.

We are constantly processing feelings and reactions although we use to do it in an unconscious way. In fact, the behavior of our interlocutor can reflect what he perceives through our non-verbal signs in terms of our attitude, our feelings or our beliefs. Hence we people react in accordance to those perceptions, propitiating a situation where we will feel right to say *"I don't know what you refer to"* or *"I don't know wherefrom you draw such ideas"*.

Obviously, an answer of this kind is not a great help to making some progress in the conversation.

What we want to say, dear reader is that we have to assume the responsibility at least for some aspect of the interpretation made by our interlocutor. It is true that there is the possibility that the interlocutor is reacting from his own sensibilities or his preconceived ideas, although it is also possible that probably there are some authentic elements in what that person perceives.

Because of it, instead of categorically shoving back the perceptions of the interlocutor, it would be preferable to approach the situation with assertiveness. I.e., showing empathy first, then exposing our point of view and, finally, proposing a joint action.

- 1.YOU – empathy (active listening)
- 2.ME – my opinion (based on facts and on my feelings)
- 3.WE – an offer for joint action

Key sentence

It is preferable to say something like *"I don't feel comfortable although I don't know why"*, **than trying to conceal what our non-verbal communication will betray anyway.**

The fact that we show disposition to consider the validity of the perception of our interlocutor obviously transmits the positive message that we value and consider as important the feelings and the perceptions of that person. This proceeding underlines the importance that respect has for us and actually is part of empathy. Besides, it is possible that our interlocutor is just right...

ELEMENTS OF A COOPERATIVE PROCESS IN CONFLICTS SOLVING

The investigation on the motives and behaviors that lead to the conflicts or that promote them, strongly emphasizes the transcendence of the "irrational emotions".

Besides, perception is also very important in relation to those motives. It is always necessary to have in mind that the perceptive distortion of the interlocutor is practically systematic in any situation of conflict.

We all tend to perceive our own behavior in a more benevolent and legitimate way that the Other's behavior. It is a basic psychological law.

As well, we also have some special inclination to assume that "the Other" perceives our behavior the same way as we do it.

The parts in conflict, in general, reduce their level of communication, with which they also diminish their ability to mutually understand each other. This lack of communication increases mutual antipathy.

All these mechanisms are especially visible within groups. Concretely in what we call "groupal thinking", a kind of thinking which in many cases is the result of the internal pressure of the own group. In groups we tend to have some very stereotyped visions of the rivals, which leads us to not even negotiate.

To generate the conditions where a constructive process of conflicts solving may take place, we should introduce in it the fundamental elements of a cooperative process:

- Good communication

- Sharing the information
- Confidence
- Mutual respect
- The perception of the similarities in values and in beliefs
- The acceptance of the legitimacy of "the Other"
- A process centered on the problem

In some cases, the strategy of problems solving cannot be put into practice until legal procedures –or in their defect, coercive measures– are put into play to attract someone initially recalcitrant to the process.

As we have seen, one of the characteristics of any conflict is that the concrete problems tend to expand into some much more generic and bigger problems, with which the relation between the parts tends to end up deteriorating. In those cases, disagreement drifts toward sheer personal antagonism. At that moment, we shift from criticizing or labeling a concrete behavior to centering on the person. We accuse the person; we talk about his character, intentions and motives. Instead of centering on the problem at hand, we think that the interlocutor is actually the problem. Obviously, from this point on it is very difficult to backpedal.

It is interesting to observe how, in this process, more and more people join the playfield. Actually, when the parts are aware of their impotence to achieving their aims, they start looking for allies ready to take part in coalitions or in supporting groups.

Also it is habitual that, at some moment, the conflict stagnates. At this point, it might be said that the conflict has reached a maximum point of intensity and then it is difficult for the things to go worse.

People involved in the conflict starts pondering the need for maybe collaborating with his interlocutor. This doesn't mean that the parts "should get along well", but let's say that they start to being mutually accepted. This is essentially due to the fact that there comes a moment where the tactics lose efficiency and the resources (the energies) exhaust. Quite often, the parts also lack the social support that they were initially possessing. Or they suspect that the cost of the conflict will be so high that it must be avoided by all means.

In those cases, "saving face" is a psychological mechanism related to the process of stagnation. None of the parts is ready to change his attitude first. Because of that, the stagnation will last until one of the parts, or a third one, manages to deactivate this mechanism and then the de-escalation may begin.

COMMUNICATION IN CONFLICTS

As we see, besides following a structured process, the success of conflicts management depends to a great extent on the establishment of a good communication with the counterpart. In this respect, it is good to be conscious that when communicating with "the Other", there is a series of factors that favor communication and another series of elements that difficult it.

FACTORS THAT FAVOR COMMUNICATION:

- Be good listeners (encourage the interlocutor to speak of himself)
- Be interested in the interlocutor in an authentic way and talk to him about what he is interested in
- Do that the interlocutor feels important (and do it in a sincere way)
- Speak always with respect and with a positive attitude
- Unclasp the points where we agree
- Try to see things from the point of view of the interlocutor (beside seeing them from ours, obviously)
- Use phrases that express desires and preferences, instead of requirements (for example, "*I would like to* ...")
- Communicate at different levels (at the level of facts, of opinions, of desires and of feelings)
- Ask the interlocutor for opinion

- Formulate open questions that induce to talk
- Use direct questions that request specific information when we want to obtain concrete information.
- Try that our communication is clear and tidy

MESSAGES THAT HAMPER COMMUNICATION:

- To criticize, to reproach or to defend ourselves from a critique by counter-attacking
- Interrupting the one who is speaking, or making too extended declarations
- Being hostile or aggressive (doing sharp commentaries, using sarcasm, etc.)
- Giving orders or making statements like *"you should"* or *"you should not"*
- Making generalizations (*"you are always complaining"*)
- Ignoring the messages from the interlocutor (for example, swapping conversation topics whereas the interlocutor wants to continue his own line)
- Apologizing unnecessarily (this propitiates that the interlocutor loses respect)
- Trying to indicate what our interlocutor thinks or feels, speaking in his behalf.
- Giving advice out of the blue

In consequence, any process that we follow to manage the conflict will have to bear those essential communicative aspects in mind.

Request changes of behavior

When we want to approach a conflict directly and we think that we have all the information we need about it, many people prefer approaching the matter realizing direct critiques.

We don't use to keep in mind the fact that the majority of people use to react very badly when criticized. The critiques trigger in us feelings of hatred, of resentment, of anxiety or of low self-esteem and use to estrange us from the person that expresses them.

Most investigators indicate that those adverse reactions before the critiques respond to our craving for a good self-image. And obviously, when people criticize us we see this self-image endangered.

Therefore, the critiques are not effective for modifying behaviors and, in fact, very often the criticized person, instead of improving it, ends up worsening his behavior.

We are all aware of that impact. Maybe because of it, many people use to inhibit before behaviors and/or attitudes that should be tackled with no delay and prefer to tell people what they cannot stand about them. Other times, on the other hand, we are so generalist – by fear that the interlocutor perceives our commentary as a "destructive" critique – that we don't manage to offer him some valuable information so he can identify the specific behavior and, therefore, start looking for possible solutions to the conflict.

We, actually, differ from this negative vision of the critiques. In our opinion, constructive critiques exist and moreover they are tremendously necessary. Another thing is to bear in mind that to realize them there are two fundamental requirements: that both the person that criticizes as well as the one that receives the critique are mature persons (remembers what we have exposed about the "adult"?). Both parts must have very clear in mind that the only intention of any critique is to help the one that receives it (or to encourage him in order that he improves something) and, at the same time, help improving communication and personal relations.

In any case, given the natural trend to react badly (or, at least, unduly) before the critiques and to confuse a constructive critique with a destructive one, in many circumstances it turns out to be more important to replace the critiques by what we call requests for a change of conduct.

How can we ask for those changes of behavior? There is a series of stages that it is necessary to cover.

Stage 1: Detect the problem

The first question to ponder is if we face a problem caused by the inappropriate behavior of the interlocutor, in order to determine whether it is appropriate to request the behavior change in that person. For this we have to bear in mind several things:

- If the behavior of this person is harming our rights or those of other people
- If we think that what we are going to ask him is realistic (maybe we think that "the Other" cannot change some type of behavior)

- If this person may feel harmed. If it is like that, we have to foresee what consequences can stem from this reaction, both in the short term and in the long term.
- If it is really important that the interlocutor changes. If the inconvenience caused by his behavior is quite slight or if we think that it is very improbable that such a behavior happens again, we might consider that maybe it is not worth requesting the change).

STAGE 2: EXPOSE THAT WE HAVE A PROBLEM

When exposing a problem it is important to briefly present the concrete behaviors that we cannot stand and that we wish to see changed.

It is important to stress that we are the ones that have the problem, provided that, in the end, our needs that are not satisfied. On the other hand, it is more effective that we express the problem as ours, provided that otherwise the interlocutor may perceive that we are accusing him. If we accuse the interlocutor of being importuning us (or if perceives it so) undoubtedly he will go on the defensive. Therefore, when presenting the problem as ours we have more probabilities that this person "helps" us solve it.

Equally, when describing the behavior that we cannot stand it is convenient to:

- Specify the concrete behaviors
- Ask him to change only one behavior at a time
- Avoid disqualifications, critiques or accusations
- Avoid generalizations (they don't use to be exact and they tend to put our opponent on the defensive). It is much more efficient to put forward concrete and recent examples.

- Don't presuppose that the behavior of the interlocutor is loaded with bad intentions (for example, just to get under our skin)
- Stay serene and calm (avoid showing yourself aggressive or insecure)
- Show a non-verbal language coherent with what we say (calm but firm, neither aggressive nor inhibited)
- Pick the moment and the place adapted to realize this request of behavior change. It is crucial to be alone with the interlocutor.

Stage 3: Make him see the impact of its behavior

Later, we can explain our interlocutor what has happened or what may happen as a result of the behavior that we want him to change. In other words, the negative consequences that this behavior has for us or for other persons. For example:

"I have a problem. When you yell at me in front of my collaborators I believe that you give them very bad image and that they may lose respect".

Stage 4: Describe how we feel

It is about exposing the feelings that arise when the person expresses the very behavior we want him to modify.

Once again, it is important to express our feelings without attacking the interlocutor and, as we were saying before, without presupposing that bad intentions exist in his behavior. Our aim is neither to be hostile, neither to generate any more controversy, or to put the interlocutor on the defensive; we just want that person to change the behavior that we cannot stand.

Precisely, as we have seen, maybe one of the most relevant keys to success in the most delicate situations is to disconnect ourselves from the emotional part of the brain and to connect with the rational part. When done so, we should be capable of formulating a simple but at the same time powerful question: "Am I really acting the very way I wish?"

Because of it, the following reflections can be of great help when the conversation starts failing:

- Let's ask ourselves, what do I really want? (For me?, for "the Other"?, for this relation?)
- Let's ask ourselves, how would I behave if I were acting like I really do wish?
- Later, let's behave as we wish.

STAGE 5: LISTEN TO THE POINT OF VIEW OF THE INTERLOCUTOR

After expressing the negative impact of the behavior of the interlocutor and exposing our feelings it is critical to keep silence to make possible that the interlocutor intervene.

The ideal thing is that the interlocutor proposes the solution or, at least, that he collaborates to find it, as he will then be motivated to carry out the behavior change that we propose him.

In no few occasions, our interlocutor has just not been conscious that his behavior produced a negative impact on "the Other" and, when realizing it, shows interest or comprehension and even manages to offer a solution to nuance or to eliminate the behavior that we have exposed as unsatisfactory. In this case, we would be explicitly grateful for this initiative and would end the interview at that point.

In other occasions, nevertheless, people respond putting themselves on the defensive. This proceeding could be due to the way we have presented our arguments (have we been sufficiently rational?, have we left aside any type of aggressiveness in our words?), but beyond this interesting analysis (thinking about how we have done it can constitute a good learning to adequately manage future conflicts) undoubtedly we have to confront this defensiveness.

The way of doing it is to be clear and express that what we want is that the interlocutor stops showing some behavior. In the end, that's why we are speaking with him / her. Actually, it is not convenient for us lo let the emotions untied in this conversation; hence we will choose to listen empathically to the arguments or the feelings of this person. By doing so we are recognizing his right to see things in a way different from ours.

Now, we will repeat our previous argument:

"*I understand perfectly your point of view although when you yell at me in front of my collaborators I believe that you give them a bad image and that they may even lose some respect*".

It may happen, all in all, that our interlocutor doesn't show interest for the problem we are raising or that he doesn't propose any solution. In this case, we move onto the following stage of the process.

STAGE 6: ASK FOR THE WISHED BEHAVIOR

If the interlocutor doesn't propose us any solution that seems minimally acceptable, we must be the one that proposes it, specifying with clarity what we want:

"*When you shout at me in front of my collaborators I believe that you give them a bad image and that they might lose respect. I would like that from now on, when you have to tell me something, you do it without screaming and privately*".

Moreover, in order to make our offer more attractive and convincing, we can highlight the positive consequences it has for both if we accept that proposal. For example: "*This way we will get along better and I will be able to modify that very behavior you cannot stand*".

If in this moment the interlocutor shows a favorable attitude it is important that we reinforce it expressing our own positive feelings as "*it makes me happy that you understand it*", "*I am grateful that you have listened to me*", etc.

STAGE 7: RESOLUTION

Come to this point, very limited possibilities exist. If the person with whom we are speaking offers us a solution that is satisfactory for us or he accepts our offer, we proceed to be grateful for this intention and we will decree the interview finished.

If the agreement we have reached doesn't appears completely clear, it is good to reformulate it to verify that both parts have understood the same thing.

If the person rejects the offer, the most effective thing is to appear empathic with that person and to try to understand his point of view. Also, we can insist on our request reminding him the positive consequences that the proposed change would have, along with the negative consequences of his current behavior.

We believe in the general kindness of people (more or less), but we are conscious that inevitably the reader will stumble on persons that, by means of stratagems, will try to prevent and ignore his desires.

What can we do in those cases? One of the possibilities, placed in this context, is to use the skill called "the scratched disc". This assertive skill consists of repeating our point of view coolly, without being drawn away by irrelevant aspects:

"Yes, however..."
"Yes, I know that, although my point of view is..."
"I agree, however..."
"Yes, however what I was saying..."

LibrosEnRed Publishing House

LibrosEnRed is the most complete digital publishing house in the Spanish language. Since June 2000 we have published and sold digital and printed-on-demand books.

Our mission is to help all authors **publish** their work and offer the readers fast and economic access to all types of books.

We publish novels, stories, poems, research theses, manuals, and monographs. We cover a wide range of contents. We offer the possibility to **commercialize** and **promote** new titles through the Internet to millions of potential readers.

Enter www.librosenred.com to see our catalog, comprising of hundreds of classic titles and contemporary authors.

www.ingramcontent.com/pod-product-compliance
Lightning Source LLC
Chambersburg PA
CBHW030241170426
43202CB00007B/77